WHEN I BECAME A
MAN

A Perspective On Manhood, Life And Relationships

To

KENNY

From Mommy

DEREK T. TRIPLETT

DEDICATION

This book is dedicated to my phenomenal children, Destanni and Donovan, who have seen me grow as I watched them grow up. Also to my late grandfather, Tommie L. Triplett, Sr., who I wish could have watched me grow up and try to reach his stature.

ACKNOWLEDGEMENTS

Thank you, Lord, for unending love, forgiveness, and favor.

A sincere thank you to all of my family for your undying love
and unwavering support.

To the staff and parishioners of Hope Fellowship Church,
Daytona Beach, Florida. I love the Family of Hope.

To Robin, my longtime assistant.

To Sherri and all TCO staff for your work
and guidance on this project.

To all of the fans and listeners of the *Making Changes*
radio broadcasts. You pushed me to put it on paper.

To John, Kevin, and Vikki. There is nothing like having people believe
in you when you are doubting yourself.

To Jackie Hicks and the Fond Memories Photography staff.

To those who never stop praying for me.

To all who help me grow.

To all of the boys and men whom allow me to help us grow together.

To the one who says, "Get busy on the next one."
So many smiles, so many miles.

When I Became a Man: A Perspective on Manhood, Life and Relationships
by Derek T. Triplett

© 2015 by Derek T. Triplett

For information, address:

The Church Online, LLC
1000 Ardmore Blvd.
Pittsburgh, PA 15221

International Standard Book Number: 978-1-940786-31-5

Library of Congress Catalogue Card Number: Available Upon Request

Scripture quotations marked (NIV) are taken from the Holy Bible, New International Version®, NIV®. Copyright © 1973, 1978, 1984, 2011 by Biblica, Inc.™ Used by permission of Zondervan. All rights reserved worldwide. www.zondervan.com The "NIV" and "New International Version" are trademarks registered in the United States Patent and Trademark Office by Biblica, Inc.™

Printed in the United States of America

First Edition, December, 2015

Trademarks

All terms mentioned in this book that are known to be or are suspected of being trademarks or service marks have been appropriately capitalized. Use of a term in this book should not be regarded as affecting the validity of any trademark or service mark.

Table of Contents

CHAPTER **ONE**

Responsibility and Recognizing the Need to "Man Up"

HAVE YOU EVER FELT ON THE EDGE?

The man on the edge has a certain look. If you have any interpersonal skills at all, you know it when you see it. It comes in different versions, but each time, there are the same familiar features. It is actually a picture I would prefer not to see at all, but one I have unfortunately seen all too often, and…at times, while looking in the mirror. That's right; I know of what I speak. I, too, have been there.

Sometimes it is a constant angry expression. No matter what is going on, the "man on the edge" looks angry. Other times, it is that lost look in his eyes. Sometimes it is represented by drooping shoulders and a hung head, shaking in disbelief or defeat. All of these are sure indicators that the brother is on the edge, and most times, with good reason.

Times are hard these days. Men feel the pressure to excel and to stay on top of every situation. In these tense political and economic times, that pressure to stay out of trouble or to stay focused on goals regarding family, friends, and self is intensified. I know those who are older or of past generations are saying, "Times have been hard before." That is true, but we were not prepared for the challenge and chaos to this degree. Most of us are products of previously successful generations, who enjoyed economic growth or expansion and developments in race relations, gender equality, and national pride. We have also not been conditioned for the level of stress and chaos that we experience now; the environment is in trouble. The world is warring on all levels, and it's not just world wars. It's all civil wars, crimes against innocent citizens, and border wars that affect numerous countries. This generation, currently trying to make a living and prosper despite setbacks, went through great prosperity and good times in past years only to have the bottom drop out again and again. In some cases, people are simply not equipped. Men, as head of households with certain expectations in society, are particularly affected.

For some, the trouble starts with a lack of education or of marketable skill development. In this world of challenges, how can they possibly compete? Or so they think. For others, it is the lack of resources, jobs, and career opportunity. Plenty of us have skills and energy to offer, but the opportunities on the surface seem few and far between. Many men in particular have negative habits they can't break, a past they can't live down, the right woman they are struggling to keep or the wrong woman they can't seem to get rid of, or children they don't know how to raise or struggle to care for financially. For them, these men with the weight of the world already on their shoulders, the stress, the perceived failure, or even the fear of failure is more pronounced because they are the supposed head of the household, the breadwinners of past generations, and the strength in the family. For some men, it is difficult to work and strive for higher positions and stay proud and confident when on top of their struggles, society says they also must play roles for which many have not been equipped or have no example of in their own lives. To equally share with the child's mother the daily responsibilities of life and children, housework, homework, cooking, problem solving, and emotional support on top of a couple of jobs catches some men ill-prepared. When times get tough, men are the ones to blame and the ones responsible for making things better. To top it all off, many men have not been groomed to be strong. There is this thing called "the heart." It doesn't come from a woman, a wardrobe, a reputation, or from carrying a gun and simply acting tough. A man with no heart is going to struggle to effectively manage life in today's society, especially with all of the challenges and complications presented to us these days. Heart is intestinal fortitude—inner strength. It is the ability to push forward despite difficulty or pain. It is the strength to conquer fear, have courage under fire, and overcome your limitations. Heart is what makes the weaker, smaller guy win or die trying against the bigger, stronger guy. Some men do not have it, and eventually, it shows.

A man with no heart is going to struggle to effectively manage life in today's society, especially with all the challenges and complications presented to us these days.

Are you feeling overwhelmed? I completely understand. Trying to do the right thing all the time is exhausting. Many are simply tired of fighting the mental, physical, and emotional grind. In the not too distant past, there was a degree of prosperity that made us all a little too comfortable. The present times and the lack of preparation for the challenges are doing a number on many men. What can be done? We cannot wait for times to change. We have no control over it. All we can change is ourselves. That change can start with a shift in attitude, mentality, and focus.

I know some who are reading this are already saying that bit of advice is typical and trite. Maybe. Maybe not. Nonetheless, it is true and helpful. A good attitude in bad times will stand out. It is healthier and doesn't cost you anything but some motivation and discipline. A good attitude has to have an internal source so that it is not controlled by external factors. There is a place in you that has hope. There is a part of you that trusts the good in people or, at least, gives them the benefit of the doubt. Find those places and build on them.

A good attitude in bad times will stand out.

We all have these places where hope lives. If we are feeling ill-equipped in one area, then we need to find our areas of strength and tap into those. If a man finds that he is not the best at dating, then he should do the work to fix the problem. If he is simply in the wrong relationship, he should move on and do so in the most respectful way by letting his significant other know how he feels and what he must do. Honesty requires bravery, and if, for example, we can create movement in our personal lives, we can certainly move other aspects of our lives forward, such as our professional lives. If a man is feeling challenged at work, then he needs to communicate that to those close to him and, if it is safe or appropriate, to his superiors and to himself. Again, honesty is the right path to bettering oneself. Once a man can clear his head and get himself on the right track, other aspects of life fall into place. Suddenly, he is able to prioritize his skills, his tasks, and his life in general. After all, if he can be honest with the woman in his life and get his relationship on track or be honest with himself and force himself to interface with his superiors at work, then he can certainly talk to his loved ones, get his family life in order, or become a leader in his community. These are the places in which he should excel. These are areas in life that, once prioritized, can be under his control in a positive way.

Now, how do we as men shift our minds upward? How do we do that consistently or daily in the face of all those daunting challenges? I'll tell you how; we can consciously fill our minds with better things. Think of it as fuel or food for your mind. Just like we eat healthy foods and adapt certain behaviors to become more fit, the same is true with our minds. We need to feed ourselves better thoughts and expose ourselves to more positive and more diverse experiences. We can all read more, or even ask outside our regular circles of guys who play weekly basketball at the gym or the guys at the water cooler at work to broaden our horizons and suggest good books or new music. We can engage enlightened people at church, in our local diner, or at the community's museum. We can watch better shows on television or no television at all. We can remind ourselves that most things that are meant to entertain are not meant to inform, and we can think outside the boxes that contain us most of the time.

If we all get a new focus, at first we can change our lives through perspective, and eventually we can fully change how we live. We may not even change what we are viewing; we might just change how we are viewing it all, which can be enough. We need to actively get off the edge and focus on the positive, the good, and the important. We can't let anything, with little or no qualitative or quantitative value to us, dominate our focus. As men, we know that inherently we need to execute our respective plans. We need to live in a positive manner with our families, our communities, ourselves, and God.

TOUGH VS. HARD

None of this transformation and growth is going to be easy. Growth is actually for tough guys. In fact, who is the toughest guy you know? Does he appear to be where he wants to be? Growing up, we all knew tough guys. Maybe some of you were one of those guys. I wasn't. I had to fight the tough guys to survive and keep my respect. You know the fellas I'm talking about, though. They ran the playground, the park, and the neighborhood. If you weren't one of those guys, I'm sure you can still remember some of their names, regardless of how long ago those days have been. Certainly, we can all remember the tough guys of the movie and television world.

None of this transformation and growth is going to be easy.

I remember when I was a kid and my dad and I would watch the Clint Eastwood *Dirty Harry* movies; the consensus was *this dude is tough*. The 70's and 80's were the eras of the tough guy movies. Charles Bronson, Richard Roundtree as Shaft, and Sly Stallone as Rocky were some of those well-known tough guys. I also recall watching Muhammad Ali vs.

Joe Frazier fights and thinking Joe Frazier was so tough. But when Ali beat him, what did that say about Ali? I don't think we ever viewed "The Greatest" as the toughest, but Ali was, indeed, tough. Now, most of these tough guys weren't mean for the sake of being mean. They had credibility, a sense of justice. They commanded respect because they earned it. They fought for what they believed and, often, for what was right.

Back in the day—in my day anyway, which wasn't that long ago and definitely set the tone for what exists today—women were apparently impressed by these tough guys. Why? Because they were sensitive to what was right and tough enough to prove it. They wore their toughness on their sleeves. A number of years ago, there was a song called "Tuff Enuff" by The Fabulous Thunderbirds (1986, Dave Edmunds, Producer; Kim Wilson, writer) that told the whole story. The chorus repeats the question, "Ain't that tough enough?" The song references everything from fighting a grizzly bear to walking ten miles on hands and knees or putting out a burning building and working 24 hours a day and seven days a week. The verses seem funny now because this is not necessarily how we approach women these days or how we prove our "toughness" in everyday life. However, it does illustrate how intentions and the poetry of words can be enough. The new life or perspective we talked about previously including new music, new attitudes, and a new outlook on life is precisely what some of these tough guys were striving for. They lived life the way they wanted to and they fought for what was right, including their women, their opinions, and their way of life. Moreover, they were proud of it all. There was a sense of poetry and sensitivity in their words and actions.

In thinking back on such lyrics and ways of thinking, I wonder: Is the "old school" "tough" for men the same thing as today's "hard"? You hear that so much now among younger men: "I'm just hard," or "Man, you gotta be hard; don't let nobody punk you." "Hard" is now a look, a style of dress, a demeanor, and an attitude. Hard is about your ability to represent, demand your respect, and survive in the "hood" and the streets. If that is the narrow definition or description of hard, then I think there is a contrast between yesterday's tough and today's hard. They are not the same. As a matter of fact, I think we need more tough guys than hard guys. Again, the tough guys are what I think we should all try to be in that they are sensitive, honest, hardworking, dedicated, and in demand.

Today's "hard," as it is seen in our neighborhoods and portrayed in television and movies, has some necessary positive components missing and seems to be directly opposed to some other very important qualities. Whether it is absolutely true or not, hard, as it is promulgated, often comes across as unnecessarily narrow and anti-intellectual. This is unfortunate because some of those who depict that image are some of our most brilliant brothers. We see this attitude and demeanor depicted by our modern day poets and musicians or talented athletes and role models. However, in some cases, their brilliance is not being conveyed or transferred to much of their consuming audience. Being hard seems to say: I have to walk around mad all day. I have to be insensitive to women. I have to challenge and rebel against all authority. I can't actively pursue an education and I have to limit my vocabulary I have to conform to other media-driven stereotypes. And I surely can't be seen openly worshipping God.

Whether it is absolutely true or not, hard, as it is promulgated, often comes across as unnecessarily narrow and anti-intellectual.

A while ago, one of my deacons was discussing some of the aforementioned pop culture hype. He is around my age and his formative years, like mine, were in the 70s and 80s. He said to me, "That's not manhood; that's just 'hood.'" Again, it might seem trite, but I have to say, he is somewhat correct. That type of hard has nothing to do with becoming better, living the best way you possibly can, or being tough in life. But, it has everything to do with simply surviving in a rough neighborhood, putting up defenses to appear strong, or covering true selves so that the poets, the fighters, the true tough guys, or the leaders cannot emerge. Once, my son said to me, "Daddy, Ice Cube can't be respected as a gangsta rapper after doing the movie *Are We There Yet?*" Has Ice Cube lost his "hard card"? I think he has been tough enough to figure out how to expand his career, create more lucrative revenue streams, tap into his creativity, and employ more people. I'm sorry if he lost some "street cred" in the eyes of innocent, inexperienced people, but for those of us looking for adult or general role models, he did what he needed to do.

I'm not hard; I don't have the look, the walk, or the demeanor. That's not my "stylo," as my sister would say. I am tough, though. I have had to be, for life has been tough. Yet, with the help of God and the support of family and friends, I've not only made it this far, but I praise my God that I'm making a contribution. Like so many of you, I'm tough enough to make a difference. Our boys are being taught to be hard, but in some cases, not tough. A lot of guys behind the clothes, the look, and the gun are actually soft. Don't let it be true for you. Be true to yourself, expand your horizons, look beyond what feels safe, and be honest and strong enough to leave hard behind and become tough: ready to face whatever life can dish out.

My grandfather, Tommie Triplett, Sr., was tough, but I would not call him hard. For example, as I said before, Muhammad Ali was tough, and Mike Tyson was hard. There is a big difference. Martin Luther, Martin Luther King, Jr., Malcolm X, Jackie Robinson, Jim Brown, and Earl Campbell were all tough, but I wouldn't call them hard. They were all hardworking, dedicated, and earned the respect they received. As I said, too, tough men excel against the odds. They take care of their responsibility and accept and conquer the challenges of life. They get back up when they fall. They raise their children. They impact their communities. They stand up against injustice and oppression. They go to work and swallow their pride when they have to because they have mouths to feed. They work and go to school if necessary so they get their families out of the hood. Tough guys do homework with the kids, spend real time with their one woman, and they worship and serve their God. As my spiritual son, Larry, would say, "Come on, tough guy." Tough guys negotiate and don't just resort to trying to eliminate. They can be found everywhere. They are in churches, in boardrooms, in businesses, on bad jobs, in line for jobs, in politics, in music, in sports, and at school. They are on Main Street and Wall Street. There is one that presently lives at 1600 Pennsylvania Avenue named President Barack Obama. The toughest guy I have ever read about is Jesus of Nazareth. With the help of God, he took on the religious, political, and spiritual worlds all at the same time. Then, defeated, was put to death and eventually escaped death. He was a tough guy. If only I could be more like any of these people; if only all of us could be more like Jesus. With a little discipline, we can.

Tough guys do homework with the kids, spend real time with their one woman, and they worship and serve their God.

DON'T KILL YOURSELF:
THE PHYSICAL IS AS IMPORTANT AS THE SPIRITUAL

Of course, all of this does take discipline, but we all have to do what we can in all aspects of our lives without overdoing it. I'm in a place right now where I'm starting to have new dreams, and I encourage others to do the same. In freeing our minds and expanding our experiences, as I suggested earlier, we often afford ourselves additional opportunities and despite thinking these little steps are trite, we find new successes and happiness. In my case, as a result of prayer, positive thinking, and forward movement in life, my present situation has changed significantly, and the future is bright in Christ. As one of the favorite songs I have ever written says, "My best days are ahead of me." I don't know the complete plans of God. I'm not even sure of all I want to explore regarding the final grand plans in the near future because I'm so happy exploring the journey now.

Personally, I'm coming out of some of my comfort zones, which is what I'm asking all of you to do in this chapter. There are so many variables in anyone's life. There are so many things that require our attention: ministry, business development, further education, and our kids and their pursuits. We combine these with the need for strategic balance to achieve personal success and fulfillment. Isn't this what we all face daily? Given all that I'm asking you to do in living well emotionally, is it too much to also ask that we as men make sure we are healthy and HERE to help our families, friends, communities, and churches? In this way, we are fully taken care of and ready to embrace life, responsibility, and God's plan for us.

There are two known variables that are tied to all of these unknowns in life: 1) I cannot pursue any dreams or visions if I am not alive, and 2) Maintaining good health will make said dreams and visions easier to achieve. Bad health is a limitation. Like other limitations it can be overcome, but it is nevertheless, a limitation. While we cannot control health challenges that are derived from genetic predisposition, an accident, or a sudden illness, we owe it to ourselves, our families, and our dreams to practice good health habits through diet and exercise. Beyond getting older or trying to look good, we as men all need to begin looking at what eating and exercise habits will assist us in meeting and exceeding our goals in life. Once we get a personal and emotional plan in place and once we step outside our comfort zones to enlighten ourselves, it is imperative that our physical health match our spiritual and emotional health.

The health and mortality statistics concerning men, especially black men, are staggering. Black men live 7.1 years less than other racial groups. They have higher death rates than women for all leading causes of death. They experience disproportionately higher death rates in all the leading causes of death. 40% of black men die prematurely from cardiovascular disease as compared to 21% of white men. They have a higher incidence and a higher rate of death from oral cancer. Black men are five times more likely to die of HIV/AIDS, and a staggering 44% of black men are considered overweight with 24% of the demographic as obese. Black men suffer more preventable oral diseases that are treatable. Black men have a higher incidence of diabetes and prostate cancer and a high suicide rate. In fact, the latter is the 3rd leading cause of death in 15 to 24 year olds.[1] We don't have to go to the statistics, do we? We can look at our families and see generations of hard-working men who did not take care of their health. Some have suffered from preventable illnesses that were debilitating in some instances, keeping them from family, work, friends, and community. A lot of these well-intentioned men died prematurely, leaving behind grieving or struggling families and lives left unlived to the fullest. When I'm traveling I frequently see elderly black couples and the wife is spry and fly, where the man is barely making it. How many children lose their dads without real cause? How many grandsons won't have a grandfather who is healthy enough to play catch or go bowling? Brothers, we have to do better. In many cases, we are overworked, undernourished, and out of balance with stress management. But as we established earlier, we can stop this trend—we can consciously make changes.

As I said before, I am starting to dream again. I have some new goals, even at this adult stage in my life. I know without a doubt that I have

---

1   Chicago: Black American Health Statistics, http://menshealth. about.com/od/blackhealth/a/Af_amer_stats.htm

things that God still wants to do through me. My health is a part of that. I am always reminded of the deathbed statement of the great Scottish Presbyterian preacher, Robert Murray McCheyne, who died before reaching his 30th birthday. He said, "God gave me a message to deliver and a horse to ride. Alas! I have killed the horse, and now, I cannot deliver the message." Personally, I have some things I want to do in life, and, as I said before, I encourage all of you to reach inside and find out what you want to accomplish and what you need to do to get there. Obviously, one of the key components that I am advocating is to absolutely consider putting our health first and foremost. Even at my age, with young kids and at the height of my career, I still think ahead. In line with the previous message to be a good role model, one of my biggest goals, which requires me to be tough in the right way as a man and to "man up" and do what I need to do, is to be able to take my future grandkids to the park and play on the swings one day or to take them to the beach and play beach volleyball. I want to play horse with my grandson and beat him at basketball because I still have a jump shot. For me, bad health would be an obvious limitation to those goals. Let us all do better, as husbands, fathers, grandfathers, brothers, and friends—as men collectively. Here are some things we should all do on this step to healthier and therefore more helpful and effective men:

- Get regular checkups.
- Get the age-appropriate colon and prostate exams.
- Eat better.
- Get proper amounts of sleep.

- Do cardiovascular exercise as vigorously as your body allows. Don't just walk if you're capable of doing more. Know the cardio intensity your body needs to make a real difference.
- Don't run the streets. It ages you.
- Stay off the drugs.
- If you must drink, do it in moderation and don't become addicted. (Note to my fellow Christians: I am not advocating the consumption of alcohol, but I am also clear about what the Bible says. These articles speak to all men and not just Christian men.)
- For single men: if you are not sanctified yet in your sexual behavior (and you should be), be safe and don't be stupid. (Note to my fellows Christians: We are to raise and maintain the standard while meeting people where they are. Again, these articles are to all, not just the sanctified.)
- For married men, honor your vows and remain vigilant concerning risks associated with sexual behavior.
- Find a healthy way to relieve stress.
- Know that it will take discipline.

All in all, as we take this journey "man to man" in my book, I want you to begin to examine what changes can be made in your lives to take responsibility for life and, in doing so, make a better life for yourself and others. I want you to be tough, as sensitive, strong, capable men who can raise children and support families. And I want you to take care of yourselves as men, as the head of the household, so that you are around for your grandchildren and what God intends as your role as men in this world. We are men, and we can always do better.

RELATIONSHIP
BREAK **ONE**

Making the Most of Family Time

It's a lot to take in: taking care of yourself physically to be the best that you can be, stepping up earning potential and power to keep the family happy, mentoring, and keeping in mind that young men and women are watching and we all need to be examples. It is A LOT to take in.

For most of us, family is at the top of our priority lists. If family is number one for most of us, detail here why we feel that way. If it is something else, feel free to comment on that too—why it is our top priority, how we keep it there, and why we address it as something important in our lives.

_____

_____

_____

_____

_____

Of course, because we are multi-faceted family men, we have priorities. What is our #1 priority and what priorities follow?

1.

2.

3.

4.

5.

6.

7.

8.

9.

10.

In our daily lives, how do we fit these priorities into our busy lives? In the space below, detail a typical day from beginning to end, keeping these priorities in mind and inserting them (or some of them) into the details below.

Morning: _____

_____

_____

_____

_____

Midday: _____

_____

_____

_____

_____

Evening: _____

_____

_____

_____

_____

WHEN I BECAME A MAN

In perusing these detailed lists and examinations of our daily lives, choose three attainable goals related to family and your daily priorities. List them here, then briefly talk about how you might reach each one without compromising family life, career, health, etc.

1.

2.

3.

_____

_____

_____

_____

_____

_____

_____

_____

Finally, as men of faith with family, career, physical well-being, spirituality, etc. as some of your key priorities, evaluate yourself below in three areas in which you do well. Below that, list three areas of your life in which you could improve or list three qualities you need to work on or change.

Evaluation of Top Areas: _____

_____

_____

_____

_____

_____

_____

Three Areas for Improvement:

1.

2.

3.

CHAPTER **TWO**

Pay Your Toll. Play Your Role.

BEING A GOOD FINANCIAL ROLE MODEL

Now, as we've established thus far, I have many "man-up" credos and recommendations. One key point that I feel is important to mention now is the manly art and practice of the "pay up" premise. Because men are often the family breadwinners or at least the dominant contributors (statistics report women leave the workforce more often to have children and care for them once that decision has been made by the family), and because society expects a certain level of responsibility from men, there is that added pressure we alluded to earlier, and therefore, a different level of pride. Now I know men usually don't like anyone talking to them about how they should spend their money, save their money, or handle their money unless that person is a financial advisor. Brothers, know that I mean well when I say that we have to pay up. We have to man-up and handle our business relative to financial matters. As a Christian man, I was given the following advice when I was about 21 years old: pay God (tithes and offerings), pay yourself (savings), and then pay everyone else. Paying God has been easy. The other two have been a challenge at different points of my life. Nevertheless, the plan for all of us has to be that we need to employ stricter habits about budgeting and spending in general, as those proud heads of the household.

As a Christian man, I was given the following advice when I was about 21 years old: pay God (tithes and offerings), pay yourself (savings), and then pay everyone else.

Men do tend to spend money. We shop, and we are savvy retail customers in general. This is something that we don't talk about often because, again, maybe it doesn't seem "manly" enough, especially when most retailers target women of all ages and not necessarily men. African-American men and other specific demographics tend to struggle with credit card debt and other dangerous spending and saving habits. I don't need to reiterate to you, man to man, that bad credit and debt is not acceptable when we are striving to be role models, breadwinners, and successful men of any demographic, ethnicity, or race in this world. Nevertheless, let's face it: your credit score matters. It has become almost as much a part of our identity as our social security number. In the Bible it says, "A good name is more desirable than great riches; to be esteemed is better than silver or gold" (Proverbs 22:1 NIV). In fact, in the financial arena, your credit score is your "name" and quite possibly even your reputation. Protect it. Think about it. In a marriage, a woman exchanges her dad's name or the name she has built for herself for her husband's. If her husband's name—or, in the financial world, his credit score—means little to nothing in financial institutions, then she will have to keep depending on herself or her dad in financial arenas. While for some males that is fine and acceptable, for a man-up man it is not. The credit score needs to be safeguarded and to do so, we must only create bills we can pay and pay those bills on time. So, yes, we are on retailers' radar; we are a desirable demographic for the lure of consumerism. We certainly want to strive to be someone who can provide for his family, buy his loved ones the things they want or need, and even take care of himself once in a while, but we need to be smart about it.

Beyond the retail discussions, there are a couple of bills common for men that should be non-negotiable for Christians and non-Christians alike. For the Christian, we know that paying tithes and offerings should not be up for discussion. It is a matter of obedience and reverence to God. Paying tithe to the church is something we all need to budget for as Christians. The other absolute, non-negotiable payment that applies to all (if relevant) is child support. Paying child support is a statement of our honor as fathers. As adults, we know that relationships and marriages do not always last and, as adults, we make decisions to either get counseling or to end them. Children are innocent bystanders in these cases. They also represent relationships that are separate from the man to woman relationship. Men should love their children, regardless of how they feel about their former spouses and mates. Further, all men should pay their child support, period. It does not matter what the current relationship is like with the mothers nor should we allow the actions or attitudes of those mothers to affect in any way the children and their need for support from their fathers. Pay your child support. Financially support YOUR children. Of course, as we allude to here, that is not all your children need, but beyond the unconditional love you should be providing and the promise to stay in their lives no matter what has happened to the related adult relationships, you need to man-up and pay up. We are required, as men of pride and dignity, to look out for the welfare of our children.

> ## *We are required, as men of pride and dignity, to look out for the welfare of our children.*

In general, I began this chapter by suggesting that what we do SPEAKS volumes for our identity. Financial responsibility for men in this world is huge. To take care of a family, we all need to take care of our finances and make sure that, beyond food and shelter, we can also provide comfort and support to our loved ones. As Christian men of a certain presence in society—whether we are there yet or striving to get there—we also need to tithe, and we need to make sure that, if required, our children are taken care of with child support no matter what.

HAVING A VOICE

As men of substance or men with pride and presence in our communities, we need to watch how we perform or act in other scenarios too. After all, what we say reflects who we are, and what we do defines our character for those around us. We need to picture ourselves commanding a certain respect and then take the necessary steps it will take to get to that level of respect.

I remember when I was a kid and a sporting event or television show I was watching would be interrupted because the President of the United States was speaking; it would frustrate me. That was before cable television, so there was no switching around from CNN to MSNBC or

Fox Network, and there was no escaping the message. It used to amaze me how the adults in the room would glue their eyes to the television set and listen to what the President was saying like it was the most important speech in the world. I also recall how the room would stop if my late grandfather, Tommie Triplett, Sr., spoke. Again, everyone viewed him like he was the most important person in the room. He had an inherent respect from the entire family, and what he said was taken as gold—something to heed, something to remember and respect. Of course, those of us blessed to grow up in a two-parent family, even for a while, heard from our mothers numerous times, "Go ask your father." My children have heard it on countless occasions, I'm sure. For children, it means that they need to go and ask the head of household, the guy who holds all the answers or at least commands the presence to claim such an honor. And, in truth, all of these occurrences taught me that when a man of substance and/or power speaks, it matters; it truly matters.

All men talk. We talk about sports, politics, and, of course, women. We tell the stories of our accomplishments and personal exploits. Sometimes those stories are embellished. We talk in locker rooms, on basketball courts, on golf courses, in parking lots, at sporting events, and so on. Sometimes it is serious. At other times, it is just shooting the breeze, so to speak. While all men talk, only a few men truly speak or say something that will rivet us to the TV screen to listen or stop a room full of conversation to hear what one man is saying. We all know this through observation, and there is no denying that a "speaking" man, a man truly saying something or living a life that would warrant wisdom and the sense that we must listen to him, is significant. It's hard to put

WHEN I BECAME A MAN

our finger right on what it is, but it is apparent that what these select few say is important and valued by those who have given them their "voice." Martin Luther King, Jr. and Malcolm X were the main national voices of the Civil Rights era. When they spoke, it mattered. For years, Alan Greenspan was chairman of the Federal Reserve. When he spoke, it mattered. When Vernon Jordan speaks in Washington politics, it matters. When Warren Buffett speaks about money, it matters. In the Bible, Elijah was a true prophet. It mattered when he spoke. I am blessed to be the father of two extraordinary children and the pastor of a good church that's headed for greatness. Most of time when I speak, it matters. I have tried to be a good steward over those roles so that I might maintain my voice because over the years I have come to understand the importance of that esteemed position.

A man's voice is earned. In some cases, it is awarded to him by virtue of his position. In others, because of his work and achievement. If a man's position gets him his voice, he can only keep it through his accomplishments. He must properly manage the roles and relationships that gave him his voice. After garnering respect and position by hard work and through the support of others, it only makes sense to keep those support systems and that respect alive with consistently admirable behaviors. Further, these men in these positions have the responsibility to speak if they are indeed voices to listen to.

A man's voice is earned.

CHAPTER TWO

The urban community suffers from the silence of significant men. I believe that every man who has his "stuff" together must have a voice because he does all of us a disservice if he does not speak. Often, we are devoid of the wisdom and instruction of significant men in our families and communities. There is so much going on that there needs to be instruction, advice, and declaration as well as a conversation from men who have a voice. Speak up, sirs. Speak to that child, that community, or that government leader. Communicate with other "speaking" men so that we may get the value that comes from iron sharpening iron. Then, speak with one voice and change the world as we know it.

The urban community suffers from the silence of significant men. Yet, every man is supposed to have some level of significance. While all of us are not meant to be agents of change, transformative leaders, the voice of our community, or some business financial heavyweight, all men have value and significance and should always be pursuing personal growth and development. This growth will lead to individual success and societal contribution.

There are some men who are undervalued because they do not seem "special." They are just normal, regular guys who go to work, take care of themselves and their families, and do the right thing. They live normal lives, yet many of them are to be applauded for simply being normal. Why? Certainly, we must assume that some special things have happened in order for them to be normal and settled in their calm roles as "regular guys."

In John 5:1-15, there is an episode where Jesus goes to a man who has been incapacitated for 38 years. He asks the man, "Do you want to be made well?" He then instructs him to rise up, take up his bed, and walk. On another occasion in Scripture, in Acts 3, two apostles are on their way to pray and see a man lying at a gate who had not been able to walk his entire life. One of the apostles, Peter, says to him, "In the name of Jesus Christ of Nazareth, rise up and walk." These are only two of many examples found in the Bible where men, with the help of God, have been raised to a sense of normalcy. In my opinion, we lose sight of the fact that in most of the miracles in Scripture, supernatural power is used to restore people to their normal state. Walking is normal. Sight is normal. Use of one's hands is normal. Extraordinary measures are taken for men to rise and be ordinary, and this is a good thing.

BEING A "REGULAR GUY" ON YOUR WAY TO SUCCESS

"Rise and be normal" seems like a contradiction. When we think of a man "on the rise" we think of someone who is about to do big things or as we used to say, about to "blow up." What I was talking about earlier—the men of substance who need to use their positions to be heard, to be the voices of families, communities, churches, and generations—they are also men of ordinary means. They are driven to extremes or by big changes to elevate themselves, all for the chance to be ordinary, to be normal examples for the good of this world. The connotation is that these are men who are expected to start doing some good—even great—things, but not without some training or time with the ordinary. I believe all men should have the capacity to be good, normal men. Yet, we are not all going to be great men as society defines greatness. We do not all have great marketable gifts, abilities, or talents, but good and ordinary are characteristics that should be appreciated, especially when one has had to rise up just to be normal. Many of us feel the pressures of daily life and have even let it get us down. That does not mean, however, that we cannot rise, live well, and teach others to do the same. The voice of the ordinary is just as good as the voice of the extraordinary. The men we talked about earlier who rise to lead need those in positions of great strength and normalcy in their communities to listen and follow, then lead and live life in the example of those who are good and facilitate positive change. If you are down now, you can be up in no time. If you have no direction, don't rail against those who do; instead, join them and live in tandem with your brothers who lead. Live in friendship and in example to those who need to come through that same difficult space that you once did.

The voice of the ordinary is just as good as the voice of the extraordinary.

I congratulate the brothers who are on the comeback trail. For so many, life has dealt them a bad hand, and they have not known how to play it and win. Others have made mistakes that caused them to fall. Many have been broken and rendered physically, emotionally, or financially paralyzed. They have been down: down and out, down on their luck, down for the count, or whatever other cliché one would like to use. Doing the normal things that a man would do has become an improbable chore for them. Whether it is being free from incarceration or the challenges of the corresponding record, the lack of the financial ability to legally provide for one's family, bad choices in romantic relationships, being undisciplined with one's "manhood," or the myriad of other things that can get men down, numerous men have been on the bottom for a while. They have worked hard, and with the help of God, people who believe in them, and the blessings of grace and mercy, many men are on the rise back to a degree of normalcy. Depending on where one has started, normal can be abnormal. Ordinary can be extraordinary. Regular can be irregular. For those who are rising just to walk—not to fly, just walk—I salute you, and others should as well.

Whether we are living well now and simply need to elevate ourselves financially to become the epitome of success or whether we just need to get to the point where we are honoring God and our children and families, we are united. We are men living on purpose. Whether we are men of significance and community presence or ordinary men rising up from difficult situations, we are united as men living on purpose. The strength we require for true success, wisdom, and respect is within all of us. We all just need to make sure that we are living and speaking the life we are meant to lead. What are we showing or saying with our way of life or our philosophies? Are we truly saying something that the world needs to hear?

RELATIONSHIP BREAK **TWO**

Creating a Presence in your Community

We've just gone over how to be a good financial role model for your family and friends, and now it is time to explore being a role model for that community of other men—young men—who are impressionable and/or working with the same challenges that you may have.

A friend of mine has a teenage son. While my friend was a man of considerable means, born of years of hard work, some of his son's friends did not come from such privileged households. Often, he would have all the boys over to his house for movies or football games. His wife would cook sumptuous meals or order pizzas and wings from the trendy pizza shop in the neighborhood. The kids would enjoy video games, television, a large backyard, and good food at his house. His goal was to be a good host to the boys and show them some appreciation for being such a good friend to his son over the years. He also enjoyed their company and was happy that he was able to offer them a hospitable home.

When his son went off to college, he got him a credit card with a modest credit limit on it. He told his son to use it for emergencies only and to avoid being ostentatious in his shows of generosity or responsibility to others. He raised a good boy, and he knew he would listen. After a few months, his son told him that he had used his card modestly but that he needed some extra money in his bank account to pay his bill. My friend was puzzled, thinking that he already had a couple thousand dollars in an account for his son that was supposed to last for months. When he asked his son why he needed so much money to pay off the card, his son replied that he had treated his friends to meals and games and nights out when they couldn't afford it, just like he had enjoyed in his parents' home in high school. He didn't realize that he had spent so much.

My friend was aghast. At first, he thought, how could this boy, with such a good head on his shoulders, make such a mistake? And further, why would he think that he had to show off for his friends? Finally, he thought, haven't I taught him better? Doesn't he know the difference between overspending and living within his means? Suddenly, it occurred to him; his son was emulating him. Because he was a self-made man, it hadn't occurred to him to explain to his son that money was to be spent responsibly and within a budget. Furthermore, that lifestyle had to be matched to your current means or financial abilities. In other words, how would his son know that a college student should not live like a successful businessman? As a kid, he had worked for his money, never enjoyed pizza for 10–15 of his closest friends completely paid for, and put himself through school; he emulated his hard-working father. While his son lived in his example with good grades and a good attitude towards life, he had not had the same struggles or experiences growing up.

Of course, once my friend explained to his son that his college money had to last and that he should be focused on studying and not worrying if his friends were entertained, his son understood. The point is, my friend did live his life financially responsible and as a good, hard-working, successful man who was worth listening to for advice and more. What he hadn't anticipated, however, was the fact that his son's "ordinary" or "normal" was not like his own, and he had to communicate to his son that being that regular guy was OK for a while. Striving for something had to be enough at his point in life, and working hard, living simply, and learning to be humble and go without now and then would make him a better man in the long run.

Remember: role models who are worthy of that community or that strong and vibrant voice have worked for what they have. They have tested themselves and stayed humble and task-oriented. It's OK to be that regular guy on your way to success. Get your ducks in a row, stay focused, stay financially responsible, and the good life will come.

CHAPTER **THREE**

Truth, Listening, and Finding a Cause

MAN OF TRUTH

I don't remember his name, but I remember being in his class. He was my "Introduction to Philosophy" professor during the second semester of my freshman year at Bradley University. There was a lot of reading; in fact, among the required texts was *Man's Search for Meaning* by Victor Frankl, a book I still quote almost 25 years later. While the reading list was heady and academic, the class sessions were very interactive. If this now nameless, but influential professor unearthed hidden inconsistencies in our logic or inherent prejudices that tainted our reason or perspective as we spoke, he would say, "Come on, fess up. I gotcha." "Fess up" was his way of saying, confess or admit it. It was his linguistic habit. He said it a lot. His goal was to get us to learn how to live in the realm of truth. To ignore inner dissonance, discrepancy, or incongruence between what we said and what we did, or what we said we felt and believed versus our actual beliefs and feelings, would be to tolerate fallacy. Confession or "fessing up" was the way to begin to correct what was divergent. Again, it was his goal for us to learn to live in a domain of personal truth. I've held this premise close to my heart and my mind ever since I took the class and listened to that wise man.

Honesty has to be important to a man. It is critical for a good man to live in the realm of truth. We owe it to God, ourselves, and to those with whom we are in a covenant relationship, at a minimum. The Bible says if we confess our sins, God is faithful and just to forgive us and cleanse us from all unrighteousness. To confess means to see the same way. Our sins must be viewed as God sees them. When we do so and acknowledge our transgressions, it opens the way for forgiveness and cleansing. When we confess to ourselves, we can walk in truth, which is so much easier than living according to lies. It takes too much energy and work to live out lies. It ultimately takes its toll on us and erodes our sense of self.

It is critical for a good man to live in the realm of truth.

In our relationships, truth and trust are partners that feed each other and facilitate growth and security. The absence of truth creates the presence of distrust. Trust is an essential ingredient for a healthy relationship. Honesty with yourself and others promotes and protects the health of the relationship. It is challenging, at best, to be close to someone when you cannot believe what he or she says. I once knew a person who was a professional liar. And by that, I mean someone who so elaborately incorporated lying into the scheme of her life that it was as if it was what she did at home, in her career, and in her personal relationships. In these cases, I believe if Satan is the father of lies, we can all just call people like her his assistants or his "juniors." In my experience with her, the lying wasn't just to get out of trouble; I think it was just a normal part of her personality. It was incredible. I once knew her, but it was just too difficult trying to decipher what to believe and too hurtful to continue the friendship, so we drifted apart, which I assume happened in other areas of her life too. However, this is what we can expect when we are not honest with family, friends, and ourselves.

At times, living in the realm of truth seems foreign for far too many of us. We have all grown up and have been socialized in a culture where pretense, deception, and subterfuge are most pervasive. Often, men "front" or put up false bravado to compete against each other and charm the opposite sex. If we so choose, based on our socialization and the pressures I've alluded to in previous chapters, we can easily be the pretenders, the masters of deception, and prone to embellishment and exaggeration, even hiding the truth or from the truth. It does not matter if it is a little white lie or a big bold-faced one; we need to learn to disconnect ourselves from the tendency to lie. In the end, personal integrity is at stake, not to mention relationships, reputations, and in some cases, jobs and career. I know firsthand that the pressures that make us prone to embellishment, fronting, or blatant dishonesty can also be our undoing in areas of our lives that are important to us.

Does living in the realm of truth mean that you tell everything to everyone as long as it is not a lie? Of course not. There are some truths that need to go unspoken. Everyone needs his or her privacy. Motive, meaning, relationship requirements, and agreements, along with expediency have to be considered. In other words, can I have some private thoughts that I need to work out as opposed to voicing them while they are still fresh, unanalyzed, and potentially hurtful? Absolutely. We are all entitled to exploring private thoughts and ideas that may not sound great to outside parties. We are often better for it when we can analyze and think about such things. You need to check your ethos and pathos, your belief system, and your pattern of actions. Have you ever heard of a pathological liar? Where there is duplicity, admit it—or fess up—and fix it.

Here are a few quick tips:

- Know yourself. Be aware of your faults and proclivities.

- Before you do something that you question, ask yourself, "If I do this, am I going to have to lie about it?"

- Determine that honesty is a dimension of love and respect.

- Remember when you were a victim of deceit. How did that feel?

- Live so that people can trust you.

- Be assured that the lack of integrity will catch up to you.

ARE YOU LISTENING?

While we're exploring or wrapping up the topic of truth, we should also address another big point of contention in our already stressful worlds: listening. "Men just don't listen!" Countless women have made that statement. I know; I have heard it on numerous occasions myself. Is this opinion accurate? Of course it's not, if taken literally. "Always" and "never" are usually inaccurate characterizations in any situation. In this case, the phrase has almost become a cliché. However, that does not mean that the old adage, "Where there is smoke, there is often fire," holds true. In other words, if so many different women say it about so many different men, there must be some truth even in the gross generalization.

Why are men the objects of this accusation so often? What is the basis of this perspective? I can only hypothesize since I don't make it a habit to survey a random sample of women or interview women on a regular basis; as you all know by now, I base a lot of my analysis on observation and social or demographic trends and studies. I surmise in most cases that when men appear not to listen and subsequently women make the "not listening" statement, the origin is for one of the following reasons or is meant to be said in the following ways: "My man does not value my opinion," or "My man often does not embrace my ideas," or "My man does not like me to correct him." You will have to ask the women in your life if you dare. What I can attempt to do is tout the importance of listening in general and then to women in particular. It does hold true, though. When we are busy, we may not listen because we're preoccupied, and in the long run that can appear—in any relationship—that we are not appreciative of our significant other's ideas and opinions. Again, we need to keep our egos in check, and we need to notice what is around us more often. Our job as leaders of the home, breadwinners, community advocates, and more entails listening and appreciating others.

Listening is truly a statement of appreciation for others. It is common courtesy to listen while in conversation. Listening indicates that one is not just interested in his own thoughts, words, and ideas. It is evident that one is not self-absorbed, selfish, or feeling superior if that person reaches out and listens. When active listening takes place, it affirms the legitimacy of the intellect, opinion, and feelings of the other person. We all have that responsibility and obligation to extend this polite gesture. When dealing with women, it has multiplied value. Women feel valued as equals and "cared about" when they are listened to attentively, and honestly, isn't that how we should be viewing them? Brothers, let me say without hesitation or elaboration that I hope we all view women as different from men but of equal worth; we should choose to engage women whose minds we appreciate. Hopefully we have matured to the point that "fine" is not all that matters; true men need an intellectual and emotional match, as do the important women in our lives.

> *Women feel valued as equals and "cared about" when they are listened to attentively, and honestly, isn't that how we should be viewing them?*

Listening is an acknowledgment of a lack of omniscience. Men are not all-knowing by virtue of being male. We really are not. I know someone is saying, "Is Derek Triplett saying that, as stubborn and dismissive as he can be?" I respond to that with a firm, "Yes!" I know I do not know it all or in some cases, much at all. Information exchange is a key to learning, and I like to learn. When we pay attention to others, we increase the probability of learning things we do not know. There are so many extremely intelligent people in the world. I hope that you have personal access to at least one person that you consider brilliant. No one should have to live devoid of brilliance. I know a few of those brilliant people, and some of them are female. I say that for emphasis, not because it should be a surprise. There are some women that I would love to sit down and have dinner with because of their sagacity and not their sexiness. I would love to learn from them. We should all reach that point in our lives.

When we pay attention to others, we increase the probability of learning things we do not know.

Listening is an exit from the narrow box of one's own opinions and perceptions.

I cannot afford to live in the potentially small and shallow confines of my own knowledge, ideas, and feelings alone. This is an area where gender plays a most important role. Men and women are different. We see the world differently. We approach life individually. Variation does not have to be divergent. Men and women are meant to complement each other with different points of view, helping both to see with more breadth and clarity. Together, we approach the whole of the matter. Fortunate is the man who has a female in his life who can help him see what he cannot see and hear what he cannot hear. It is a blessing.

I hope you are listening. I also hope that you are looking, seeing, and deciding where to put this expanding knowledge and energy. In all our lives, we also have to put emphasis on a greater good, a bigger purpose in this life. Applying truth, listening skills, and our own knowledge to any cause is also key to a successful and enriched life. And I know you're all saying that I've already pointed out how busy men are—how stressed we can get—and that adding anything else would be very difficult. However, we are all up to the task.

FINDING A CAUSE

On one occasion, I remember watching an NFL football game during the Christmas holiday. There was a feature on pro running back Warrick Dunn. The story highlighted Dunn's "Homes for the Holidays" program which was started in 1997, his rookie year. The program gives a single mother with children a piece of the American Dream by donating a house to them. Through the Warrick Dunn Family Foundation established in 2002, Dunn has rewarded more than 99 mothers and their 260 children and dependents a home for the holidays. After Hurricane Katrina, musicians Branford Marsalis and Harry Connick, Jr. joined forces with the New Orleans Area Habitat for Humanity to build Musicians' Village in the Upper 9th Ward. Currently, the village contains 72 single-family homes and 10 elder-friendly duplex units. These stories are truly inspiring.

Several years ago, I had a brief conversation with Dr. John Jackson, President and CEO of The Schott Foundation, which publishes the "50 State Report on Public Education and Black Males" yearly. It was clear when I talked to him that empowering black males through education is his passion and "ministry." I live in Daytona Beach, and one of the icons of our community is Dr. James Huger, who is 100 years young. He has devoted much of his life to educating youth, and for 18 years as Community Development Director, he has committed himself to infrastructure and quality of life improvements in urban Daytona. I also have great respect for a brother named Nigel Newton, who helped coach my son in basketball throughout his tenure at Warner Christian Academy in Daytona Beach, Florida. Nigel takes time and uses sports to help young boys become young men. Again, these men inspire me. Why?

They have chosen to champion causes for which they have passion. What social or kingdom cause has your devotion? What area of need, human suffering, or empowerment has your consistent commitment? Our society is clamoring for men to take a stand and champion causes. Sure, I know we have jobs, families, and educational pursuits. For those of us who are Christians, we also have church responsibilities, as I am sure those of you of other faiths have your obligations as well. Extra time is limited, and recreation is important. There is something else that could use your dedication. I am a pastor, so I have many causes that take my energy and effort as I work for the cause of Christ and community. Nevertheless, I have committed myself to two main causes. The first is the development of urban males and the second is to increase the level of civic engagement among urban citizens. I am passionate about both. I have launched an initiative called Getting All Males Equipped (G.A.M.E.). G.A.M.E. seeks to prepare males between the ages of 11 and 25 to be productive students and citizens. I also work to educate and empower urban citizens to take charge of their neighborhoods and to participate and become leaders of the social, economic, and political climate of their cities.

Our society is clamoring for men to take a stand and champion causes.

I am encouraging men to find a cause to champion. Just to name a few, there are community boards, recreation centers, youth mentoring programs, and sports leagues that need strong, honest, open-minded, and empathetic men. I do some of that now, but I am praying for new passion. I think we all should.

RELATIONSHIP BREAK **THREE**

Self-Evaluation, Listening, and Personal Involvement

Men have a lot of responsibilities heaped upon them daily, weekly, and yearly. We are usually so busy "getting it done" that intentional personal growth and development are not made a priority. We end up growing from experiences, successes, and failures. There is very little personal evaluation, critique, and improvement. Yet, looking in the proverbial mirror is important. A picture helps even more than the mirror. When we look at a picture of ourselves we see the real deal. The camera doesn't lie. The mirror and the photo help us to take an honest look.

Sometimes, it isn't easy for us to be honest with ourselves, let alone with others. There is the constant temptation to embellish stories, keep information from loved ones, or to deny ourselves a true look at what makes us tick or maintain our image.

Personal improvement, nevertheless, starts with taking a good look at ourselves and being willing to listen to others about what they see in us. Look and listen.

For many men, listening is an undervalued activity and an underdeveloped skill. Some would say we don't like to listen and aren't good listeners. Being a good listener is a trait that can infinitely assist a man's success. Listening adds knowledge. It adds perspective. It adds value. Active listening in and of itself helps to counteract any tendency for selfishness and self-absorption. When we listen to others we are showing that we can respect and appreciate someone other than ourselves.

Personal growth should end in contribution and not just achievement. Men can be reluctant to take our experiences and our interests to another level in the form of being vocal for causes important to us or dedicating ourselves to charities and movements that need our help. Once we tap into our strengths, however, it is easier to give ourselves—in honesty, in attention to others, and in charity and support.

What was the last thing you intentionally worked to improve about yourself? What was your process? What has been the outcome?

_____

_____

_____

_____

_____

_____

How good of a listener are you? Rate yourself on a scale of 1–10 with 10 being the highest.

_____

_____

_____

_____

_____

_____

How do you rate yourself as a listener? When was the last time you truly listened to someone? Specifically, how could you improve your sincere listening skills?

_____

_____

_____

_____

_____

List below some charities or causes with which you would like to become involved. Start with the one that most interests you and go from there.

_____

_____

_____

_____

_____

Detail here how you plan to become involved, contribute to, or promote the above causes or charities. Create a feasible plan for getting involved. Be as specific and as honest as you can regarding your timeline for these causes and your involvement.

_____

_____

_____

_____

_____

CHAPTER **FOUR**

The Slippery Slope of Being Articulate and "Having a Clue"

YOU MEAN YOU DIDN'T KNOW

About a decade ago, I made two very important personal discoveries that affect how I think and live. First, I recognized that I am not as smart as I thought I was. Secondly, I realized that in a broader sense it is not exactly a compliment to be called articulate. Both of these findings changed me for the better, and I'd like to share them now since we are running the gamut in self-actualization and development.

For as long as I can recall, I have been considered smart. I have always had an appreciation for learning. Through high school, I excelled as a student, always at or near the top of my class. I did not have the natural intelligence that made everything come easy, but if I worked at it, I could grasp it. College was in some ways a "little shop of horrors," an odyssey of emotional, intellectual, and spiritual intra-personal sparring. I'm sure many of you can attest to the same type of experience. I fought with myself the entire time, but I achieved a lot. I graduated in four years and left an impact on the university; in fact, I gave the student commencement address. There was no Cum Laude, Summa Cum Laude, or Magna Cum Laude, just thank you "Lawdy," as they say. I wish I could do those years over. Growth continued, and in life and ministry, I was considered one of the bright ones. I cherish this gift, and I appreciate it. I worked hard, and I feel blessed in many ways. Again, I'm sure many of you have had similar experiences or can maybe recount a great academic career, though wish for a better personal life. Maybe it's the other way around. Regardless, we all have our journey, and we all know our strengths and weaknesses.

I have always had the gift to speak, though. I discovered it early. It runs in my family. An appreciation for words, good memorization skills (they are not that good anymore), and the lack of fear of an audience have all advanced me in school and in professional endeavors. I was trained and developed in competitive speaking in high school and college, and it has carried me a long way in my short time in corporate America, and in ministry. Public speaking is my thing. As a preacher, lecturer, radio, and television personality, I am speaking all the time. How many times have I heard that I am an articulate young man? Often it was to my chagrin. But, I am not that smart, as I said before; I really feel that I have been given certain gifts and worked to get the rest, as many of us have. Further, as I alluded to earlier, I have found and now firmly believe that it is really not a compliment to call a black man articulate.

Let me address the latter first. I once heard that to compliment a black man for being articulate could mean that the expectation is that he is not supposed to be—articulate, that is. In actuality, the ability to speak well should be normative. Vocabulary, reason, and articulation should be basic for every adult without disability in those areas. Gender, race, ethnicity, and/or background should not have an effect on those basic abilities. Allow me to elaborate. In my opinion, there is a difference between my gift to speak and my choice to be articulate. I make the differentiation in order to keep myself in check and to make sure I do not stunt my own growth. To allow someone to make me feel special about something that is not truly special could ultimately hinder me. I should not let myself feel extraordinary for having an ordinary capability. Some brothers are choosing not to work on their ability to communicate, which is a detriment to them individually, socially, and beyond in the long run. So many men have such potential that is left undeveloped simply because they believe their strengths lie elsewhere or they are so good at one thing that they don't need to explore anything else. We will delve into this further later in this chapter after we explore another aforementioned issue—that of intelligence.

So many men have such potential that is left undeveloped simply because they believe their strengths lie elsewhere or they are so good at one thing that they don't need to explore anything else.

Until a decade ago, my history had been that if I put in the time and effort, eventually I would be on top or near the top of anything I chose to tackle. Achievement, accomplishment, and solutions would surface with a little time and effort—the same time and effort, mind you, that I always put into things. Then, all of a sudden, I found myself not on top or near the top anymore. I knew why but could not figure out a remedy. Intelligence stopped leading me to achievement or problem-solving. Life became a maze that I could not figure out. Aspects of life that I felt I once had handled became problems I could not solve. I needed ability and intelligence that I felt I did not have. The church where I pastor needed me to be a brighter, more effective, and efficient pastor, and I did not—and in some cases, still do not—have the tools and skills to do so. To my Christian readers, prayer and the work of the Holy Spirit are presupposed and present, though not explicitly mentioned here. During this period, God became truly my source and not just the resource that empowered the gifts and abilities he gave me. I looked to Him for answers when I didn't have them; I pondered over gifts that I did or did not have and used His spiritual answers to guide me in what I did next. It was apparent to me that all the intelligence and charm in the world would not give me what eluded me, what puzzled me. That spiritual growth is such a blessing. The discovery of true personal capacity and the limitations that come along with it, however, can be sobering, albeit spiritually liberating.

Exposure is an indispensable tool for development and self-discovery. Over the last ten years, I believe through God's providence I have been exposed to people who are so much brighter and more intelligent than I am. Some are even brilliant. As I have said before, everyone should have someone in his or her life who is brilliant. The time I spent in seminary humbled me. There were people half my age whose depth of Biblical interpretation, theological preparedness, and plans for kingdom ministry impact were almost intimidating. I went to class and kept my mouth closed.

I marvel at the intelligence of my children and other college students who have impacted me. Wow, the kids today are smart. Business owners motivate me. They make it happen for themselves, their workers, and their customers every day. I love achievement. There are people who are so well-read and well-versed in so many diverse areas that their conversations are exhilarating. Their ability to reason and convey their ideas and arguments help to facilitate my growth—my intelligence—and how articulate I am.

The Bible mentions the need to be sober and vigilant in order to protect one's self from an adversary that seeks to devour. My two personal discoveries have promoted sobriety and vigilance. I know how important it is to balance being realistic concerning one's ability and capacity while not becoming self-limiting or getting caught in the trap of destructive pride. Every man has to know when he is good but…not that good. It is not easy to maintain that equilibrium. I am also acutely aware of the importance of proper verbal skills, especially for a man. I want to address that more, brothers, so we'll explore that here.

YOU KNOW WHAT I'M SAYIN'?

Do you remember the last time your mate said, "We need to talk"? For many, that announcement is no problem. You simply stop what you are doing and say, "Sure." For some, it brings trepidation for a variety of reasons. Unfortunately, it causes some to ask themselves, "What did I do?" The dishonest ones ask themselves, "What did she find out?" Many just simply do not want to talk because communication can be difficult for some of us. At times, it is for me. We've addressed this above, regarding how many men do "clam up" so to speak, or don't communicate any further than what is required of them. Truthfully, we all need to be prepared when anyone wants to communicate with us—personally, professionally, and spiritually. We don't want to have to cringe when someone says that he or she "needs to talk." We don't want to be closed off when God speaks to us, and to be successful, we certainly do not want to keep to ourselves professionally when we know we can offer so much to the workplace. We need to have our store of knowledge that we draw on. We need to have words to describe our feelings, and everything we do must have a verbal way to be processed or communicated—i.e. be ready with WHY you did something or WHAT you expect to have happened, etc.

Truthfully, we all need to be prepared when anyone wants to communicate with us— personally, professionally, and spiritually.

Many times, we perform good deeds simply because it makes us feel good. We do need to be prepared, especially as men, head of the household, wage earners, or family people. If we work in a food bank or help out otherwise in our communities, we should be prepared to say it is because we felt it was an area that needed help or that we saw too many hungry or needy people in our daily lives. When we are asked at work why we believe something or why we executed a certain plan, again, we should be prepared to state that it was because the company would benefit, or it was the only way to work with another colleague, or it was something that used our strengths and we wanted to highlight that. Personally, it can be trickier, but we should always try to keep our feelings in check and our ideas and words that we want to use in the front of our minds. It is how we can be effective communicators in every way.

Over the years, I have learned that there is a difference between being a good public speaker and a good person-to-person communicator. Public speaking is much easier. Why is interpersonal communication so demanding? It could be that because, at a minimum, communication requires synergy between thoughts, feelings, intellect, and verbal skills. Depending on the situation, if either is missing, undeveloped, or mismanaged there can be a negative effect on the ability to skillfully communicate. Knowledge and experience feed our thoughts. Thinking helps to clarify feelings. Words are a means of expression. It helps to know a lot of them. Often these variables, namely thoughts, feelings, intellect, and verbal skills, are troublesome to manage individually without having them all work together. Nevertheless, this feat is worth achieving.

Words are a means of expression.
It helps to know a lot of them.

Good communication skills are invaluable in relationships. Whether it is business, professional, social, romantic or parental, a man needs to have good verbal skills. I know many are the proverbial strong, silent type. While silence is golden and it is often good to be a man of few words, men need to be able to express themselves when it counts. Ideas have to be communicated to managers or employees. Agreements have to be negotiated. Mates need to know what is going on in your head and heart. Children are waiting for guidance and impartation.

GOOD COMMUNICATION HELPS IN CONFLICT

Proper conflict manage is very important. The lack of it can be detrimental to a relationship and literally life threatening. I wonder how many men have died because two men failed to effectively communicate. They could not calm their emotions and check their egos long enough to think and then speak. How many romantic relationships have been damaged because the wrong words have been said at the wrong time. The more words one knows the better he can express his anger without resorting to four letter words. In my opinion, one of the practical reasons cussing should be left out of male/female relationships is because it can be a form of verbal abuse and in many cases leads to physical abuse. Men can resort to physical abuse because they lack the verbal skills to negotiate. They then resort to force.

GOOD CONVERSATION IS REVEALING.

Talking to others prompts them to talk to you. When people speak they reveal their thoughts, feelings, and perspectives on life among a myriad of other things. Dialogue can unveil pretense. While engaged in deep conversation, people will even leak what they are attempting to hide. It is vital to really get to know people that will be a part of your life. The better you are at conversation, the more adept others will need to be. Men, we need this skill especially in our relationships with women. Talk. Find out who she is so you can appreciate her for more than just her physical appearance. If there are negatives that far outweigh her physical presence you will know to run…fast before you make a mistake.

The better you are at conversation, the more adept others will need to be.

WISE GUYS

I had to learn there is a difference between intelligence and wisdom. There are plenty of smart guys who are not wise guys (pun is intended). Is there a guy that you know who is constantly taken advantage of and you want to say, "Come on dude, get a clue"? How about the brother who you say is too old to keep doing the same dumb things over and over? Perhaps many of us have a friend who has talent, is hardworking, and who seems to get up the ladder, but cannot stay there. All of us have seen good men do foolish things and end up paying significant prices for those acts. All of these real or hypothetical men have at least one thing in common: they lack or fail to use wisdom.

What does it mean to be a wise man? For that matter, what is wisdom? If one answers the second question, then the first takes care of itself. A wise man is one who has and uses wisdom. A simple definition of wisdom is "knowledge plus judgment." Intelligence is not wisdom. Neither is education alone. Good instincts are truly an asset, but without the requisite knowledge, a man can still be at a disadvantage. A wise man has a depth of knowledge and the ability to discern. His cognition and incisiveness give him the power and perspective to make good choices and decisions in real situations and in real time. A wise man has learned what to do and how and when to do it. He even knows when to do nothing.

A simple definition of wisdom is "knowledge plus judgment."

There is a scripture found in Proverbs 4:7 (NKJV) that says, "Wisdom *is* the principal thing; *therefore* get wisdom..." How does a man get this winning combination of knowledge and judgment? Every man should want it. The payoff can be tremendous. The cost for the lack of wisdom can be equally as great. There is a belief that wisdom comes with age. That can be a misnomer, or even a fallacy. Years give us the opportunity to gain knowledge and develop judgment, but it does not happen automatically. As we get older we have more experiences. Those occurrences do not, nevertheless, necessarily impart wisdom. We can all name at least one man who has gotten older but no wiser. Some Christians would say that wisdom comes from God, and it can. I would argue that if God via the Holy Spirit is one's only source of wisdom that impartation is most likely intermittent.

Without elaboration, I would like to proffer that wisdom comes from a combination of the following sources:

1. God via the Holy Spirit

2. Experiences (both successes and mistakes) from which we have actually learned

3. Tutelage and training from wise people

4. Interaction with foolish people

Also without elaboration I would like to offer a few thoughts on the importance of wise men thereby substantiating why more are needed.

1. It is still a male dominated world, so it would help if those who have so much power also have knowledge and sense.

2. A clueless man is either predominantly a useless man or only useful as a tool or pawn for the person (male or female) who has a clue.

3. When a man continues to make unwise choices and costly mistakes, he usually more than pays the price.

4. A wise man's advice or actions usually benefits many others, including succeeding generations, for wisdom is passed on.

5. Life is more complicated and conflicted than it has ever been. Knowledge and judgment are needed for good decisions.

6. Lies and truth are often difficult to distinguish due to Satanic forces and societal dysfunction.

7. Boys need someone to follow that can take them somewhere positive, prominent, and permanent.

8. The mighty are falling much too frequently.

Intelligence, the ability to be truly articulate, learned, and open, and the wisdom that comes with it all will make all of us men successful in life.

RELATIONSHIP BREAK **FOUR**

Why You Can Never Stop Growing and Learning

DON'T STOP GROWING. DON'T STOP LEARNING.

We have all seen those television commercials where the person is trying get in shape, rent a nice car, or rent a date in preparation for their class reunion.

At the time of this writing, a committee is putting the final touches on my high school class reunion. I was a part of the East St. Louis Lincoln Senior High class of 1985. It has been 30 years since we graduated. Wow! Time flies. I am not going to the reunion. It is a little sad to say that I have not been to any of my class reunions. There are a few reasons why, but none of them are worth mentioning here. I can imagine, though, that there will be so much positive energy as classmates see each other, especially those who have not seen each other in a while. In retrospect, I wish I could have afforded myself the opportunity to experience that energy. Nevertheless, I believe as movies and television depict, there is some "sizing up" that goes on at reunions. People look at how people have changed and how they have grown. There is probably some comparative analysis.

You don't have to go to the reunion anymore for the comparisons to take place. Facebook is the new international locator. I am not one who trolls other people's social media pages. Nor do I go looking for long-lost people. I will say that people whom I was glad to hear from have contacted me on Facebook, but I really never expected to hear from them again in life. To my surprise, I have heard from people who I haven't seen since junior high. That was almost 35 years ago. So, people know what you are doing and what you look like, even if you are never in the same room with them.

What have you done since you graduated from high school? Actor Rob Lowe does these commercials where he compares himself to another version of himself. In a particular one, he compares himself to "peaked in high school" Rob Lowe. Man! It has to be awful to have peaked in high school. I understand athletes who never played in college or the pros but had great high school careers. So many peak in athletics before getting to the big time, but to peak as a person has to be disenchanting once it is discovered, or worse yet, pointed out. People are supposed to grow and not just get older, aren't they? Lifelong learning should be embraced by all, shouldn't it?

I am afraid of peaking because I do not want to be obsolete. My Dad once told me that every man fears his own obsolescence. Again, I do not want to be obsolete. Even if I didn't love learning, the thought of obsolescence would move me to continue to grow and learn. What moves you to keep growing and learning? What could move you to keep growing and learning? Let me offer some possibilities:

1. **Your crew.** If you surround yourself with people who continue to grow and learn they can push you to do the same. Association can breed assimilation. This is positive peer pressure.

2. **Intentional exposure.** Stretch yourself beyond your comfort zone. Learn the things you know you do not know. Go places. Talk to new people and go to places outside of the normal. Exposure creates new experiences and the new experiences bring new opportunities to learn and grow.

3. **Reading.** Read, read, and read some more.

4. **The Internet.** There is a wealth of knowledge on the Internet. Use it for empowerment and education and not just entertainment.

CHAPTER **FIVE**

Planning… A Man's Best Attribute?

WINTER CLEANING

When I was growing up, Saturdays had a particular routine. If my mother was home and had not worked a second job on Friday night, we enjoyed a large Saturday morning breakfast. If she had worked, we were usually on our own in the food department. One thing was consistent, however, and that was our Saturday chores. I can still hear her saying, "All right, it's time for you all to clean up." At times, it was the typical house cleaning like dusting, vacuuming, mopping, bathrooms, etc. Other times, it was more extensive such as windows, walls, cabinets, and the dreaded outdoor shed. Spring cleaning was the worst because it entailed doing the most comprehensive cleaning of all and spending all day cleaning. This involved cleaning under beds, behind bureaus, up and down the stairs, and in the closets. We also had to get rid of all the stuff that hadn't been taken care of, monitored, or cleaned out at all in months. And it's easy to forget to clean behind the beds and the bureaus all winter long. It's easy to let dust and dirt accumulate when life is busy and our focus is somewhere else. My mother had the right idea, though, to keep up with it all and to not let it get past us.

As an adult, I like to do some personal winter cleaning. It happens for me annually toward the end of the year. My mind, almost involuntarily, begins to contemplate what needs to be cleaned out before the end of the year in all aspects of my life. I start with my clothes closets. What do I need? What do I not wear anymore? What can I give to charity? I always eventually move to my home and church offices shortly after I get the clothing settled. I de-clutter rooms, do the old spring cleaning a full season ahead of time, and go through all my drawers and files to make sure that everything is in order and to throw out old paperwork and items that I don't use anymore. Before year's end, I will also even clean out my computers by getting rid of clutter and organizing files. To me, this process is rejuvenating. It helps to clear my mind and get me organized. I am able to be more creative and to project ideas for the future. When I am operating simply and efficiently, I am better. And for me, doing this at year's end prepares me for the new year ahead. I recall those days with my mother, being made to clean the whole house, and I am grateful. Because I spent all those Saturdays cleaning the house, I have become quite good at doing my own cleaning out.

When I am operating simply and efficiently, I am better.

As men and as heads of households, businesses, churches, and other areas of life, we need to be at our best at all times. I've detailed my reasons and simple, yet comprehensive, areas for organization, and I encourage all of you to do the same. How many times do we feel like we want to start a new venture, but we just can't seem to get it together to start it? How many times do we feel that we could contribute to another's success and mentor him, but we just can't provide the guidance we know is there? And how many times do we hear that people are enjoying certain financial freedoms or successes, but we haven't yet achieved those milestones despite a good income or even a marginally improved financial situation?

I maintain that, with a few simple steps—a clear, concise routine even once a year—we can all be the best that we can be in terms of organization, forward thinking, and being "clean" in certain key areas of life. As I said, each year, I simply start thinking about refining my wardrobe a bit—making room in my closet. Beyond that simple task, I am able to evaluate what I need, how I look, if I've gained or lost weight, if I've spent money wisely, if I am presenting myself in the way I want to, if I'm using my workout clothing as often as I should and more. It becomes a self-evaluation of sorts. Clearing out the old helps me move forward with new initiatives, looks, feelings, and resolutions. This simple closet cleaning, of course, leads to other, bigger organization efforts.

I then move to my home and office, making sure my files and all my affairs are in order, from the furniture I have to the items I use in my kitchen. My whole family will often get involved, and we all move forward as more organized and with a clean house that my mother so valued years ago. Once I do get to my office and my files, I feel a heightened sense of accomplishment that allows me to add other creative endeavors or professional ventures to my repertoire.

Of course, once I'm thinking professionally, and this is your opportunity to do the same, I really start to evaluate my habits and my lifestyle—again, in certain segmented areas. I check on my credit, I evaluate and clear out my contacts list in my cell phone, and I clean up my act in general.

Yes, as uncomfortable as it may sound, you do need to check up on your credit rating annually—at least. It is imperative that you know where you stand in terms of good or bad credit. If you find that your credit rating could use improvement, work to pay bills, pay down credit, and establish new, positive income sources or investments. It doesn't need to be significant investments that you explore. There are plenty of opportunities out there for self-employed IRAs, checking accounts that allow for a savings or reserve component, and more. You don't have to be rich to save your credit; you just have to be vigilant and responsible.

You don't have to be rich to save your credit; you just have to be vigilant and responsible.

Also beyond getting my computer files in order, I expand that to my cell phone. This is a practice I borrowed from a friend of mine. I will regularly go through my cell phone and delete the numbers that I no longer have a real reason to keep. It does not mean there is a conflict or any other kind of problem. The cell phone actually serves as a relationship metaphor. There is only so much storage capacity on our cell phones. We need to keep the available space for those with whom we remain in a real relationship with whether it is business, professional, or personal. Real relationship does not necessarily mean consistent conversation, but it does entail mutual contribution and benefit. If those two components remain, the person stays. If they no longer exist, then why keep the number? Again, this is good practice in relationships too. Let go of the old or those that are not beneficial—sometimes even detrimental—and bring in the new. New opportunities, new people, new places, and more.

Of course, finally, as I clean out my closets and my files, I turn to myself and my behavior. I ask those hard questions: Am I doing the best I can do? Have I been the best person, husband, father, friend, etc. that I can be? For me, I evaluate annually in a very formal way, and a year is a long time. During that time, any of us can lose our edge or get off our games. Mistakes happen. Wrong choices can be made. We can give too much attention to some things and neglect others. Bad habits can develop. They don't have to be sinful, immoral, or egregious, just counterproductive. The end of the year is the time for personal examination. If you are like me, there are some things about you that you cannot take into the next year or even the next phase of your life. Sometimes they are small things, and other times they are initiatives or changes that you (or I) have been putting off for a while. Regardless, make time to clean them out!

SAVING IT ALL UP

Of course, by this "saving" I do mean, very pointedly, saving up your money. I strongly feel that once everything is organized as we discussed previously in this chapter, other aspects of life and organization of that life will fall into place. Saving, however, does take some effort, and as I touched on above, is imperative to do; it is completely linked to that aforementioned credit rating and our financial success and stability in life. Several years ago, I remember reading an article about what was then a potential NFL lockout. DeMaurice Smith, National Football League

Players Association Executive Director, sent a letter to NFL players that said, in essence, a possible NFL lockout was almost certain for a recent year. He also advised the players to save their money in order to protect their families. What a concept! Saving money is a part of protecting your family. Spending money is notoriously perceived as a part of satisfying or spoiling our families, but saving it is actually a big part of protecting our families. Again, as men, this task often falls to us, and we need to step up and make it happen. Note that even in the case of NFL players, who can make large sums of money in a year, they still need to be advised to save their money. As I said: What a concept!

We recently experienced the worst economic downturn since the Great Depression. There was rising unemployment, and the housing market became crippled with unprecedented foreclosure rates. Ends are still not meeting for most of the middle class. We all know that handling money can be tricky and problematic. I have seen people on the news consistently saying that their savings have been exhausted. And to me, if these people had savings, they were doing well at one point. If someone like that is hit by the economy, what does that mean for those who were unable to save and felt that they were just getting by? What about those people with no savings? It means, unfortunately, that financial desperation or collapse is imminent.

Men, we all need to become disciplined and make saving money a habit, even if it hasn't traditionally been part of our lives. "Rainy day" funds, percentage savings, and personal investment and retirement accounts are all necessary. Our families and our financial success depend on these initiatives. It is an easy step to schedule time with a financial planner. The following steps, beyond just scheduling the planner, involve making some sacrifices and staying vigilant about your money. Proverbs 13:22 (NKJV) says, "A good man leaves an inheritance to his children's children..." To leave financial benefit for my grandchildren, I know that I will need to be disciplined and stick to the plan. Brothers, we may not be able to buy all the "big boy toys" that we want if we are going to follow the spirit of that scripture, but we have to save some money. Regarding our finances, simply put, we have to apply some discipline and stay informed.

Regarding our finances, simply put, we have to apply some discipline and stay informed.

Many people fall off the savings wagon and need to get back on it. I've been there myself. I know, though, that I have two children in college, and I don't want them to suffer with too many student loans. My daughter will get married one day, so I have a wedding to pay for, and I am sure it won't be cheap. There will be future grandchildren to help educate. Who knows when the next economic downturn will happen or how long this one will last? We all get the point. Save!

NOW THAT WE'RE ORGANIZED: WHAT HAVE YOU BEEN READING?

So, I've detailed the importance of getting your affairs in order and getting yourself prepped and ready for anything, as head of the household, by organizing files and cleaning out the clutter. I've taken that further and asked you all to get your finances in order and project for the future. Now, I'd like to revisit our intellect, our "reading fitness" so to speak, as men.

I have a few questions for you: What's the last book you read? What book changed your life? Is there one book you would recommend for all of your friends to read besides the Bible? Who is your favorite author? Do you prefer fiction or nonfiction? Do you get your newspapers delivered to your doorstep or to your iPad or Kindle? I certainly hope that you can answer at least one of the questions above—hopefully, more—and with an informed and sensitive opinion.

What's the last book you read? What book changed your life?

To those who could not relate to the above questions, I understand. I know that some might say, "I am a man's man. I don't worry about reading." That's cool. I understand that. Well, for those of us who see the value of being a little more literate, having our vocabulary expanded, and adding more depth to our conversations, I will keep writing so you—so we all—can keep reading. While I do a lot of reading because of my profession, I would not call myself an avid reader, though I do plan to be. I love the value of it. I read the daily newspaper. When I get the chance or take the opportunity to read books just for pleasure, I really enjoy it. To those naysayers, I reiterate that while I get your perspective and understand that for you, it is not part of the persona you want to project or part of what you consider important in life, I do think you should give reading a try. Granted, as men, I've said it before: we have a lot to handle.

We are often head of the household or hold time-consuming jobs, and we have a lot of pressure from family, from peers, and from society in terms of expectations. For that reason, I implore you to read. As men, we need to expand our horizons and stay smart and informed, but further, we need to relax and take time for us too. Consider the following:

Reading deepens your knowledge. Francis Bacon said, "Knowledge is power." How do I know that? I read it. The more a man knows, the better man he can be. This holds true on different levels whether he is a neurosurgeon, an NFL quarterback, or a master craftsman. They all hone their crafts and sharpen their minds by reading. You naysayers can't even dispute that.

Reading expands your vocabulary. According to the Oxford Dictionary, there are about a quarter of a million words in the English language. I don't know how many I know, but it is probably not enough. Words are needed to express thoughts and ideas. The more of them you know, the better you can express yourself. Sometimes I find myself searching for the right words to say to convey what I am thinking or feeling. As a speaker, pastor, and writer, this is important, but it is also important for all of you in your respective careers and family positions.

> *Words are needed to express thoughts and ideas. The more of them you know, the better you can express yourself.*

Reading is useful in conversation. I am an introvert. I am not a great conversationalist. I do not chit chat very well. At times, when attending functions that require small talk, books and reading come in handy. After answering the normal, "How is the church?" and "How are the kids?" questions, there is that awkward pause in the conversation. I usually fill that sudden silence with the question, "What are you reading?" People usually return the question and voila, there is something to talk about. And men, I don't mean this in a trivial way, I mean it in a "always put that best foot forward, expand your horizons, get to know people, get to know yourselves" kind of way.

In a nutshell, it is important to have yourself in order. It is important to have your family, finances, and life taken care of and handled. It is also important to put your best foot forward, because all the work you do to improve has to be communicated somehow. My advice to all of you is to read—for benefits in conversation, at your job, socially, and beyond. Men, it's all part of being the best we can be and sharing "Man to Man."

RELATIONSHIP BREAK **FIVE**

Cleaning, Planning, Saving, and Reading—A Couple of Simple Disciplines that Lead to Success

As head of households and businesses, men often have to multi-task. In doing so, they are respected and revered as in charge in the workplace or as the breadwinners and caretakers in their families. When it comes to our personal business, however, men, do we always make sure that everything is in order from our wardrobe to our finances and beyond? Do we have our ducks in a row when it comes to saving money or planning for our own personal, creative, and professional futures? Do we expand our horizons and read or participate in other activities to be the best we can be for our families and ourselves?

It is important to look put together. Our cars should be clean, our clothing should reflect the type of success we want to achieve, and our desks, our homes, and even our attaché cases and bags should always appear neat and organized so that people believe, consistently, that we are together at all times. I'm not saying to buy the most expensive clothing or to have the biggest car on the block. I'm just saying that we need to present ourselves well. In a paragraph here, I want you to detail how you feel people perceive you. Right below that, I want you to detail exactly how you want to be perceived. Then, compare the two.

_____

_____

_____

_____

_____

_____

_____

_____

_____

_____

_____

RELATIONSHIP BREAK FIVE

After reading some of my philosophies on how I stay organized, I'm sure it is apparent that I like to do a thorough annual check of all areas of my life and clean them up. I handle my clothing, my home, my office, my computer files, and beyond. What do you do, currently, to clean out or keep yourself organized? Similarly, after reading my account, what do you feel that you need to do? Detail all of that here. Again, provide each section back to back and compare.

_____

_____

_____

_____

_____

_____

_____

_____

_____

As part of our cleansing and preparing ourselves for all that life has to offer, we need to have our finances in order. First, rate your financial fitness below. Then, detail steps that you can take to make sure that your credit is improved or that you have more money put away—whatever your financial goals might be for the coming year, within reason. Again, compare where you are with where you want to be when you have completed the short paragraphs.

_____

_____

_____

_____

_____

_____

_____

_____

_____

Finally, create a reading list for yourself. As you've just heard in the last chapter, I strongly recommend reading. I want you to look around, read some reviews, ask some friends for recommendations, and create that list below. After that, detail for yourself where you are in terms of reading or expanding your intellectual reach. Do you even watch educational television? Have you seen a documentary? Do you collect old jazz records and stay up-to-date on artists? Whatever it is that you do, detail that below and think about how you might expand more on that in the coming year.

_____

_____

_____

_____

_____

_____

_____

_____

_____

CHAPTER **SIX**

The Importance of Teamwork, Looking Good, and Reflecting on What's Really Important

SHOULD YOU BE LOOKING FOR SOME PARTNERS?

What do Steve Jobs and Steve Wozniak, Bill Gates and Paul Allen, Abbott and Costello, Orville and Wilbur Wright, Johnny Carson and Ed McMahon, and David Letterman and Paul Shaffer all have in common? They were all partners of sorts, and successful ones at that. In fact, this is just a small list of men from history and present day who have joined forces to do something significant. Steve Jobs and Steve Wozniak, along with Ron Wayne, who signed away his 10% after ten days at the onset of the company formation, were the founders of Apple Computers. Bill Gates and Paul Allen are the founders of Microsoft. And, the others, of course, are broadcasters and celebrities who created fantastic careers and followings simply by working together.

Men often think that they have to do everything on their own, particularly when it comes to achieving success in this world. However, men have been able to accomplish great things with partnership and teamwork. Individual success is possible. Yet, I have a statement that I often say and adamantly believe: no one is at his or her best entirely on his or her own. It takes a team to even cause an individual to be at his best.

We have all heard that no man is an island. Most men are just better and more productive when there is another who partners with him or pushes him. After all, synergy can be better than singularity.

We have all heard that no man is an island. Most men are just better and more productive when there is another who partners with him or pushes him.

As men, we team up in sports, business, and entertainment. I'm sorry to say that, in my profession as a pastor, true partnerships and teams do not happen very often. Ego gets in the way, as does the inability to get things done when opposing or similarly strong personalities get involved. Of course, in my business, I minister to a lot of people, and I manage quite a bit, so I need to get things done. Therefore, in business—specifically, church business—I often eschew or chase away the possibility of partnerships. In my business, it seems that there needs to be a superior and subordinate. As we all know, authentic partnership requires that we view people as equals or, in the case of business, in line with the percentage of investment, or bottom-line, a favorable financial and professional outcome. For me, although I can't quite figure out how to make it work professionally, I do try to learn from what makes other partnerships and teams work. I also apply it to other areas of my life. Maybe some of you have similar stories.

We all grew up with a healthy appreciation of partnerships and teams. As I said, we all watch sports and observe the team dynamic there. Plus,

CHAPTER SIX

I grew up watching Batman and Robin along with the Super Friends, The Lone Ranger and Tonto, and The Three Stooges. My older brother really liked Abbott and Costello, and Dean Martin and Jerry Lewis. These were all teams of mostly men, all of whom needed each other and were better together than they were apart. In my individual opinion, our communities and churches need teams of men who can drop the egos and establish, create, rejuvenate, expand, build, and eliminate where necessary for mutual and ultimately collective communal and societal benefit. I believe hip hop artists have it right with their constant collaborations. It benefits that genre of music artistically and economically, and for me, it becomes a great metaphor for what we need to accomplish or move towards in the world of church communities and pastors. Perhaps some of you can attest to this in your own churches at the lay level or even in your own professional organizations and places of business. It happens to everyone on occasion, but for men, the ego thing can get in the way—on the football field, basketball court, boardroom, coffee shop and, yes, even in church. And when I hear about failed partnerships or collaborations, it always seems like ego got involved. I heard about the canceled Jay Z tour a while back and attributed it to the artist with whom he was trying to collaborate and perform. I had seen him collaborate successfully with others and this one time, it just didn't work out. And men, it can work out. Sometimes, being the bigger person—the more "in control" person—means deferring to another, all for the greater good.

Remember, too, men, that teaming up with someone else allows you to take advantage of complementary and supplementary skills and talents. Of course, regarding that bottom line we referred to earlier, the all-important assessment of how successful these unions are, this "bundling" of skill sets, is a surefire strategy for success, both for formal and informal unions. I remember seeing a commercial where the developer of a product was in the warehouse on the phone with his partner who was making sales calls. The salesman had gotten his first buyer. He told his partner, "You keep making it, and I will keep selling it." They did not have the same skills, but they needed the individual skills of each man to make money. The production was an art—a planned and choreographed skill set, if you will—and so was the ability to sell. They were different but equal. No man has all the skills and talents, and maybe success is being held hostage due to someone trying to be a "one-man gang." Partners can benefit from the talents of each other and protect themselves from their own deficiencies.

> *Remember, too, men, that teaming up with someone else allows you to take advantage of complementary and supplementary skills and talents.*

Men, I know how hard it is to ask for help sometimes. As heads of households and breadwinners—all things that, again, society tells us are important and inherent to our existence—we often feel that we have to handle everything on our own. Teamwork, however, can provide a much needed experience with camaraderie and companionship. Honestly, in my attempts to implement teamwork in my own profession, I have to say that it is a great thing to truly have someone else in there with you, someone who has just as much invested and just as much on the line. Your beliefs, desires, aims, and motives are in unison and harmony. You are able to share in the mental and emotional sides of the process. There is someone who understands and can motivate, challenge, and encourage you. They "feel you" because they are in it with you. There is almost no stopping a superior talented team that works together and for each other with one goal in mind.

Goals for men are paramount to even beginning an exercise or endeavor, whether alone or with others. As I mentioned before, men do have trouble working together due to issues with ego. Of course, any time you have people interfacing closely and trying to work together, there is the potential for conflict. It does not necessarily have to destroy partnerships if men are mature enough to handle them correctly. We've been discussing how critical to success some of these partnerships can be, so we need to protect how we approach them and how we interact within them. A key to handling conflict is determining what type of conflict it is. Core or foundational conflicts will probably not be resolved. They should inevitably keep brothers from even becoming partners. 2 Corinthians 6:14 talks about not being "unequally yoked." If there are base differences in character, belief systems, philosophy and ethics, then he is most likely not the correct choice. Do not partner with someone you cannot trust. Situational conflicts, on the other hand, simply need to be handled with honesty, humility, positive confrontation, and negotiation when necessary. This takes maturity and the commitment to purpose over emotions and problems. As men, again, I think we can handle this and make it a simple part of our ways to improve our lives and our ultimate successes.

MAKE SURE YOU HAVE SOME GROWN MAN CLOTHES

As you know, I like to be direct and approach things simply and practically. The previous installment on partnership is a simple premise, yet one about which I feel strongly. I firmly believe that simple, easy steps to being more open about teaming up with men personally and professionally can be beneficial—a definite win/win situations in only a few simple steps or using a few minor changes. I have also been upfront about simple and easy changes to appearance, point of view, social skills, and more in this book. Now, I feel that once the idea of setting aside ego and working with other men has been approached, I can open the door to talking openly about how we look and present ourselves. And, men, those of you already shutting down and saying, "Clothes are for women" or "style is not for men," I plan to prove you wrong on both counts.

As men, we don't always admit that parenting fills your life with wonderful memories. One of my fondest recent memories was a really simple thing that happened a couple years ago. I was preaching in Miami and decided to take my son with me. We were in the bathroom of the hotel suite both looking in the mirror and tying our neckties. That's it. That is the memory. I felt like a million—no, five million—bucks. My baby boy was then in high school. The little guy that I saw come into this world, carried, put in car seats, and taught to ride a bike, shoot a basketball, and dribble with his left hand was standing next to me as we tied our ties. Right next to me, man to man.

I remember showing him how to tie a necktie and giving him a day or so to learn it. He did learn, of course. During that time, however, his favorite items of clothing were basketball shorts, t-shirts, and basketball shoes or slides, so it took some convincing to make him even want to approach learning how to dress nicely, let alone tie a tie. After a little work and discussion, I convinced him of the importance of a man being well-rounded when it comes to wardrobe. Sure, a man can fall back on his beloved athletic wear, but a man should also be able to dress well for all occasions. To me, it is important. I feel that it shows reverence, respect, success, awareness, and a whole bevy of clear and respectable looks for men. All hold their place in his success—in school, with women, with peers, professionally, and on and on. I am happy to say that, finally, my son has found his look and style and knows how to dress. Whether it is casual wear for college, business, or semi-formal, he can put it together—suit, shirt, tie, jeans, urban sneakers, or whatever. I so firmly believe in good grooming and how it makes us appear to others and how it makes us feel as hard-working, proud, successful men, that I will teach him more about the quality of fabrics and about shoes later when he graduates and is making his own money. I feel that strongly about personal presentation. I mentioned ego earlier in a negative light; now, I want to point out that a little ego, a little confidence, is a good thing.

Why, you might be asking, is this worth mentioning here? Why, after talking at length about working together for added success, would I even approach personal grooming and clothing? To me, while we are on the topic of success, it is a must in terms of mentioning and explaining. Men, you have to know how to present yourselves; you have to know how to dress. And honestly, we can all admit it; not many men have learned to be well-dressed. I recognize that for some, their lifestyle deems being dressed up or even well-groomed constantly unnecessary. But in general, we have become, on one hand, extremely casual, and on the other, outlandish. It is important to know what is contextually appropriate attire. It is also essential to know where and how to shop so that a brother can dress well on a tight budget. A man should be able to "hook up" his wardrobe. I remember hearing the comedian, Sinbad, say that a man should not have to sit on the bed and wait for his wife to pick out his clothes like he's on the way preschool. A man can dress himself and should know by design, by experience, or by educating himself how to find clothing that suits him and how to wear it. Beyond that, my only advice is to seek help from peers and industry professionals or look around on your own to find a sense of style and presentation that fits you. As I said, that ego that keeps us from working together should at least serve to make us want to feel good about ourselves and look good for professional and personal advancement. It really is that simple.

Real women still respond to a well-dressed, well-groomed man. The right clothes help in job interviews also. This is not a "how-to" commentary, but it is a "need to" portion of my book, strategically placed while we're all examining our egos. You can always get someone to teach you or assist you with this style I'm suggesting; I just want to make sure it is on our radar as men. Family and friends taught me how to present myself. My grandpa taught my dad. I laid the foundation and provided an example for my son. He will pass it on. Some men wear clothes; others have style. I obviously prefer the latter, and I urge you to make that part of your plan for success too.

Some men wear clothes; others have style.

CHAPTER SIX

SAY IT OUT LOUD

There are very few opposites that are as clear-cut as open and closed. Very few men are completely open or totally closed. I know I am neither, and I do not believe I would recommend either. Some say they are open books. I do not know if I necessarily believe that. On the other hand, I have known the strong, silent type, the ultra-stoic. But, I have seen that character of man be "broken" by a grandchild. In my opinion, the wise place is somewhere between completely open and totally closed with a man being skewed toward healthy openness. While we are on the topic of personal expression and expansion, I'd like to discuss the topic of how we individually express ourselves now. It seems to follow that, once we have our peer dynamic in place and our personal style at least in consideration, we should move to how we emotionally, creatively, and conversationally present ourselves.

Composing music is very cathartic for me. It is my way of releasing some of my most personal thoughts and emotions. Whether I am writing worship music, Gospel music, or relationship music, I tend to express a lot of my heart and mind. I think all of us need a place and/or mechanism to release what is on our minds and in our hearts in a positive way. Whether it is through art, writing, conversation with a trusted friend or professional counselor, we need it. Without that place, men can become or remain closed, out of touch with ourselves, and unintentionally, intra-personally dishonest because we have not explored enough to know the truth about self.

I want to grow as a person and not just get older. My desire is to develop as an individual and not just age. A part of becoming deeper, broader, and wiser as a man is healthy expression. This is not a commentary on how men should get in touch with their feelings. I'm not that dude. That is not something I want to write about. Nevertheless, I deem it important for men to have that place where we can be open so that we may be able to effectively process deeper thoughts and emotions in order to grow, develop, and be understood. We need that place.

I am a very private person. This has been a challenging chapter for me to write. Why? It is because in the right scenario with a trusted person, I can be very expressive. So while writing I have been trying to find the balance between helpful, honest personal communication and visceral verbal bleeding. I do not want to say too much or say too little to be helpful. Yet, I know how important it is to not be a completely closed man. It takes too much work. Other people are not afforded the opportunity to be close to you and really know you. For some, it can lead to the neutralization or slow erosion of emotive capacity. I try not to give a lot of direct advice, but sirs, find a trusted place and a healthy method to tell your own story. I don't think we'll all become "Renaissance Men" overnight, but we are well on our way.

RELATIONSHIP BREAK **SIX**

Why Partnerships, Conversation, and Putting Your Best Foot Forward are Never Minor Details for Men

I have a friend who had long lived with stories of his father's notorious poker games. His father, a local business owner, used to get some of his neighborhood colleagues together and play a weekly game with a group of professors from a local university, also from the neighborhood. The group played for over 40 years, loyally showing up at their host's house with chips and soda and petty cash—coins and small bills—simply to enjoy a game and companionship with lifetime friends.

My friend used to come over to my house and tell me that the men were at it in the basement again. His mother had brought down some sandwiches, and he himself tried to get a glimpse of the game, but as always, he only heard the sound of his dad and his friends' laughter all night long. We used to wonder what kept them interested in this game for so long. What was the draw?

Years later, my friend had just gone through a divorce, and he was feeling lonely. He never really came out and said it, but I knew he often ate dinner alone or stayed late at work to avoid going home to an empty house. He had always been a private guy, and he shot down any of my attempts to have him join my colleagues and me for lunch or a pick-up basketball game after work. He also had given up on going to professional group meetings because he said they made him feel uncomfortable.

One day, he came to me and confessed that he was tired of having nowhere to go, that he did crave the input of other professionals in his office, and that he wanted to be more social and outgoing, even well-dressed and perceived as a man in the know, or at least poised for new friendships and experiences. What had always made him comfortable, however, was reading, so he asked me if I would like to join a "Book Group" to discuss everything from *Wall Street Journal* to the latest *New York Times* bestseller, or the latest album/DVD from a whole list of artists he enjoyed listening to. I agreed to join, and I invited some of my own colleagues to join us.

Monthly, we would pick a nice restaurant and meet for dinner, drinks, and discussion. All of us dressed nicely, all of us poised and ready to meet new people. In time, we would meet even if we didn't have a book to discuss. We would dress up, so to speak, and prepare ourselves to enjoy a nice, long meal. After a while, those of us who had been strangers to one another were close friends—close enough that we could sit in silence with no awkwardness, and familiar enough that we could ask about one another's children, wives, jobs, and more.

It occurred to my friend and I one day that we had become his father and his friends, that mysterious group of men who met consistently and enjoyed one another's company for what, it appeared, was no reason. Little did we know then that years of companionship and collaboration both personally and professionally would, one day, become a draw and a constant in our own lives as well: a positive interchange of ideas, ego-free, and man to man.

CHAPTER **SEVEN**

Living as a Role Model
(Like Dr. Martin Luther King, Jr.)
and Preparing for Life's Opportunities

THE LEGACY OF DR. MARTIN LUTHER KING, JR.

In the United States, the third Monday in January is a national holiday. It marks the celebration of the birthday of Dr. Martin Luther King, Jr. As you all know, countless articles, books, and tributes have been written about, to, and for Dr. King. There have been pieces done on him since many, many years ago when he came on the national scene with the Montgomery bus boycott. Over the years, we have all studied him and his philosophies. Little children have turned in paragraphs in schools across the country. People have made movies about him. Discussion groups have been started just to examine his life, and classes have been taught at universities all over the world. He was a great man.

As high school or college students, we've all written essays and orations on him. As I mentioned before, articles and books, some that have even won Pulitzer Prizes, have been written about him, and every year we honor him on his special national holiday. Dr. King has been, should be, and will continually be a literary subject written about incessantly.

Over the years, I have drawn many ideals about leadership and manhood from reading books, watching documentaries, and listening to King's speeches. I feel strongly that many of us can learn from him, even if civil rights, politics, or other professions that keep one in the public eye are not our areas of specialty. We can learn from his bravery, commitment, and perseverance. We can also learn from his ability to stick to his point of view no matter what resistance or push back he received. And, as men, these are important qualities to gain from our examination of Dr. King. Many times, when we are reading these articles or addressing his notoriety and success in certain circles, we forget that he was simply a man with a cause, a dream, and a lot of drive. Although well-educated and extremely gifted, those attributes were tools in his toolbox as he worked to change America.

Now, certainly, I recommend that you study Dr. King and read all the works you can about him and by him. Studying him as a man instead of a historical icon or civil rights pioneer allows us a different perspective. When we take away the public persona and try to see him for who he was, we can see more clearly the personal traits that may have led to his ultimate success. We can also perhaps apply these to our own plans for success in our lives.

Again, as men, the pressure to be successful or highly regarded can sometimes outweigh the need to develop ourselves and begin to understand our own strengths and how to apply them. Dr. King started his life with a sense that he wanted to be an educated man. He went through years of school to reach the level that he achieved. Beyond that, however, he also had conviction and a strong sense of right and wrong.

He used his inherent fortitude and sense of self to apply that morality to his community. In turn, his initiatives went national and eventually international. In the midst of all his success, he discovered other strengths that the public responded to like his fantastic ability as a public and motivational speaker and his presence in a crowd or at an event. He was not a big man in stature, but he was big in so many other ways; he had intelligence, personality, conviction, and impact on his community.

He was not a big man in stature, but he was big in so many other ways; he had intelligence, personality, conviction, and impact on his community.

If we look outside our own worlds, I'm sure we can find men who inspire us. I know, as men, we can dig deep and find strength within ourselves, not to mention strengths and inspiring qualities in other men, that we may not always notice or think about as mentors or role models. After all, in our own worlds, we feel that we always have to be the strong ones, the breadwinners with our lives in order, with bills paid and futures set in stone. We are often so enmeshed in work, money, and maintaining a certain lifestyle for our families that we do not tap into our own potential. Consider looking at men in the arts for inspiration to be more creative in your own lives. Read an author who you've never read previously and find out more about him. Look at our world leaders, beyond your own doorstep, and find someone who inspires you. Of course, it doesn't hurt to look closer to home as well or into the past to see if there are historical figures who may not have caught your attention before. But now, as you're looking for expanded inspiration, they seem intriguing.

Dr. Martin Luther King did exemplify the qualities of a man who overcame odds to be one of the most inspirational figures of our time. He knew inherently that God often gives us more than we plan to handle in life. He embraced that, and he made a huge impression on this world. Properly inspired, I think we can all do the same. As I said earlier, for the good of the community and our world, we men do need to find something significant beyond our families for which we can care and take a stand. It is, after all, important to be a man of principle so that we can all determine who we are individually and understand why and how we do it.

Dr. Martin Luther King did exemplify the qualities of a man who overcame odds to be one of the most inspirational figures of our time.

Earlier, I alluded to the fact that Dr. King was brave, and he was. He was not without fear, however, because no one is. He did fight the fear, moved past it, and managed it to become greater than maybe even he thought possible. We can all do the same. We can fight fear and other obstacles that keep us from achieving what we want. As human beings in general, but especially men who have families who expect so much of them, our legacy is important. What we have done and what we have left behind does impact our families and, if given the right opportunities, can affect our communities and so much more. And this goes for both men and women. We can both see traits in Dr. King that could apply to our own lives, and we can take our own talents and move initiatives forward for a more widespread impact. What we do at the local athletic club to support teenage athletes, for example, can turn into a program, a community plan, a difference in the lives of at-risk teens. What we do with a charity through our office can turn into a better life for one family or more and can even become a lifetime initiative for the company which employs us. It is not how long we live; it is what we do with our time on this earth, and the sacrifices we are willing to make for the common good.

BE PREPARED

I have a great fear of being unprepared at the wrong time and, consequently, missing an opportunity. I think that it is possibly a fear that we should all have in healthy doses. Certainly, I'm not suggesting that we let the fear of being unprepared consume us, but, above, I did mention that Dr. King overcame his fears, and we need to do the same. In that analysis, I also implied that, for men, the potential for fear is great; after all, there is a lot of pressure on us at all times in our respective societal roles. My fear of being unprepared comes from an incident back in my teen years that, at the time, I let blindside me and caused me to miss a tremendous opportunity. Some opportunities do not come a second time. I vowed never to let that happen again, and I have spent years trying to figure out how to make that happen, to keep my eyes open and my mind open to anything so that I might take advantage when the time is right. It has been said that success is when preparation meets opportunity. A friend of mine who passed away several years ago, Lee Norris Rayam, once said that when opportunity knocks, the unprepared person would not just fail to answer the door, that person would not even hear the knock.

A number of years ago, during the 2008 Presidential election season, I was having a conversation with a friend. I was challenged regarding why I was voting for my candidate of choice. I gave my reasons, which only invited more questions about my knowledge of the candidate's platform. Little did I know that although we did not agree on who should be the choice for president, my debate "opponent" had read much more information on my candidate's platform than I had at the time. It quickly became obvious that I was not prepared for such a substantive exchange. In such a benign, but important, conversation at the time, I learned a couple of lessons. First of all, there are some people who will not allow you to get away with surface remarks. And two, cursory reading, without truly digesting the content, can get you in trouble with well-read persons. Of course, we all hate losing debates, so again, these are minor lessons to learn, but are nevertheless important in their far-reaching impact and potential.

In fact, everyone, regardless of gender, should make it common practice to be prepared. Whether it is with the mundane or the important, do your best to stay ready and on top of your game. It can be a challenge, though simply because preparation takes planning and foresight, which don't always factor into our busy lives as parents, employees, students, or spouses. Life gets in the way and suddenly, taking care of aging parents and getting kids off to college takes precedent over your own well-being, just as babies and toddlers and rising up the corporate ladder did years before.

On countless occasions, I have been less prepared than I should have been due to lack of planning. At the beginning of this chapter, we talked about a great man—Dr. King—who seemed to never have been unprepared for anything on his radar. When he wanted to accomplish something, he did, or he tried. How many of us can say that we never dropped the ball on an initiative, or we never put off something that should have been done immediately? Not many of us. In fact, most of us will procrastinate or simply not make time to take on vital components for a happy and prepared life.

In my life, there was a period of missed meetings, incorrect attire for the occasion, agendas that could have been more developed, and schedule conflicts that could not be resolved all because of lack of planning and organization. As a single person who had recently lost my executive assistant of over a decade, I could make many excuses for that period of my life. Instead, I took the reins and pulled my life into control. It started with small steps. First, I took a breath before I headed into any situation. I made sure I was calm, dressed well, organized, and ready. I also began to write my schedule down and track progress on projects and initiatives. Soon, I was moving to actually organizing my surroundings and planning ahead for everything from lunch with friends to business meetings. I am still working on planning vacations. I realized that with some changes in my life, preparation would require more planning on my part, especially with the increased demand on my life and the lack of available help and support. In turn, my need to overcompensate for a lost assistant or being responsible for myself as a single person made it possible for me to become more organized, together, and prepared than I had ever been in my life; and I have not lost momentum. It can be a struggle at times, especially when I keep adding things to my plate without eliminating anything.

Many times, we are not trying to be disorganized; we are trying to keep everyone else on track and end up forgetting ourselves. It is important to manage all of the various inputs and stimuli that can keep us from planning and, thus, ending up unprepared. Think about it. Life is fast-paced. Technology has made life easier while also creating increased interruptions. All day, there are emails, text messages, phone calls, Facebook notifications, tweets and more, and those are just to your cell phone. To properly plan, at times, it is important to hang a "do not disturb" sign on your total being so you can work on being prepared. In other words, step back and take that breath that I alluded to earlier. At times, we can be busy being busy. My hope is to be less busy and more productive. I have noticed that when I take the appropriate time to plan, productivity rises. Being too busy can be costly, though sometimes, we fall into that trap of thinking that busy is good and busy means productive. Again, take that step back, that breath, and simply take stock of what needs to happen to lead you to preparedness in life.

At times, we can be busy being busy.

Over the last few years, I have had a recurring dream. It happens to me at least twice a year. In the dream, I have had a full day of preaching, and

I arrive at my last preaching engagement for the night. I do not know the type of service or the venue. It is the last engagement of the day, and I am tired and just want God to bless the people through me in a hurry so I can retire for the day. I arrive at the venue and discover there are thousands of people there, and the "who's who" among black preachers are present, including my dad. I arrive just in time to preach and am ushered straight to the podium only to discover I have no Bible, notes, or tablet, and I am too exhausted to remember my message. I fumble through some simple Biblical oration at a time when I need to be at my best. Of course, as I said earlier, I have a fear of being unprepared. In my dream, or nightmare, rather, I was too busy to be prepared. The realization in the dream hits me right away and grips me with fear. Again, Dr. King was seemingly always prepared. If anything, we can all try to live in his example. Remember, over-extension can negatively affect preparation.

Preparation requires tools and in my nightmare, I had forgotten my tools. You cannot be prepared without the right tools. I think this premise has broad application. Ask yourself important questions that apply to you. What do I need to have more upward mobility in my chosen career? What should I be doing to prepare for this changing and shrinking job market? Which social graces need improvement? How can I be well-read so as to improve my vocabulary and knowledge base, especially on current events? Is there something missing that can make me a better husband so as to improve my marriage? What do I need to do to be more adept at fatherhood? The list goes on and on. You need tools in your toolbox. Build them and use them. In the beginning of this chapter, as we examined Dr. King, I mentioned that his ability as a public speaker was astounding. This was one of his most valuable tools and I urge you to find yours.

You cannot be prepared without the right tools.

RELATIONSHIP
BREAK **SEVEN**

Taking Inspiration from Men and Learning to be Prepared for Anything in Life

Dr. Martin Luther King, Jr. was a leader in every way. What ten things can we learn from him as men and women who strive to be leaders in our families, communities, and the world? List them here (and remember, they don't have to be prevalent qualities; they can be more personal observations).

_____

_____

_____

_____

_____

_____

List here, men, ten influential people in your lives. Make them both genders and in different professions, from different walks of life, etc. Women, do the same. In the list, detail why you feel these people are impactful, inspiring, or important.

_____

_____

_____

_____

_____

_____

_____

_____

_____

_____

_____

As part of our cleansing and preparing ourselves for all that life, as men, has to offer, we need to have our finances in order. First, rate your financial fitness below. Then, detail steps that you can take to make sure that your credit is improved or that you have more money put away—whatever your financial goals might be for the coming year, within reason. Again, compare where you are with where you want to be when you have completed the short paragraphs.

_____

_____

_____

_____

_____

_____

_____

_____

_____

_____

What step by step process can you take in your own lives to tap into your own talents? What do you need to overcome or enhance before setting out to fulfill your dreams and ambitions before you make your big contribution to the world? Close your paragraph with what you think your mission(s) would be for the world.

_____

_____

_____

_____

_____

_____

_____

_____

_____

_____

How prepared do you feel for what life has in store for you? In what ways do you feel that you are prepared for life's lessons? What steps do you take to make sure your life is orderly and organized? In what ways do you think you can improve? And, finally, what do you fear or feel when you think about facing the unexpected?

_____

_____

_____

_____

_____

_____

_____

_____

_____

_____

CHAPTER **EIGHT**

Prayer and Presence

I am not really into bumper stickers. And if you know me by now and how fastidious I am about other aspects of life, then you would know that I really do not care for putting things on my car. They become dated and tattered; the "look" of the automobile is affected. While I do not use them, I do pay attention to them and understand that, on another level, they have been carefully chosen by the people behind the wheel of those cars. There is something about whatever particular saying on the stickers that they want the world to know about them. There is, in fact, one that has been around for a while and always gets my attention that says "Real Men Pray." This statement, although seemingly benign, lends itself to much debate and argument within each nuance of the saying. For example, what defines a real man? Is there a standard for a "real man"? And, further, what part of that standard is objective? Is there subjectivity involved in determining what is a "real man"? What part does spirituality really play in masculinity? Finally, how do we differentiate what is distinctly Christian from the world's generalized definition of spirituality? The Biblical, theological, and social debate that could surround the phrase "Real Men Pray" is endless. For me, at the core of it all is what defines a "real man" or a real "Christian man." I know what defines me in both respects, but I wonder if others have similar self-awareness.

To put it simply, I need to pray. When anyone seeks to be a good man, manhood can be tough. Leadership is not always easy, as we have discussed thus far. For many men, the emotional and financial responsibilities of family combined with the pursuit of career and personal goals can be daunting at times. And that is before you add the effect of ego attachment to success in those areas, which we have also discussed. Men have been socialized to believe that they have to be successful or at least look it. They must do better than the next person, even if it means to live beyond their potential. Further, they are physically pre-disposed to being more competitive and aggressive in their plan-making and execution of those plans. It is good to get or to insert a little serenity into these busy and stressful lives. I am living proof that, in pausing to pray, I reconnect with myself and with God. It is usually just what I need to make it through my week or even my day.

When anyone seeks to be a good man, manhood can be tough.

When I am overwhelmed by responsibility and by pressures, I have learned to turn to God in prayer and recalibrate, so to speak, so that I can gauge priorities. It is in prayer that I remind myself that I live to please God, and that, as a strong Christian man, I am capable of handling anything that comes my way. I am disciplined, and I understand that this book presents a lot to add to your "to do" lists in terms of how to live or how to get your lives under control and onto a successful path. Yet, I do believe that prayer can be part of that discipline, that daily checklist to make sure that we are on track and living life to the fullest and to the best of our abilities. Again, especially as men, but for women too, we need to understand our own abilities and our own fortitude, discuss or verify it all with God, if you will, and keep on that often stressful but always blessed path to success.

In truth, too, I need to know that the buck doesn't stop with me alone. I'm too finite and fallible to not recalibrate with God on occasion. I find security in the fact that God is greater than me, and His power continues to extend when my ability has reached its end. Like I said, life can be hard, and it can get us all down. Life can also be great and challenges can lead us to great things. I find that sitting back in prayer and running it all by God is a cathartic thing for me. I can see more clearly what I need to do in terms of priorities—where I need to worry, where I need to work harder, and where I need to offer praise and thanks for what I have.

When one seeks to be a man of purpose and power, he has to frequently, if not constantly, deal with pressure. That man, the one who wants to be successful and live to handle hard work and responsibility, lives with the burden of expectation. As they say, pressure can make diamonds, but it can also burst pipes. For me, prayer keeps the proverbial pipe from bursting. When I kneel, stand, sit, or lie down in prayer it helps relieve the pressures of life. I don't have to be father, pastor, bishop, community leader, or anything else other than God's son needing His presence and help. That is a load off! It allows me to view my day—my world—in a fresh and renewed perspective. I can suddenly handle the pressure. I can suddenly make decisions that, before my prayer sessions, seemed beyond me.

We all have moments during which we feel that things—life, in general—are beyond us. Certainly we feel capable. In fact, we are capable, but we overextend ourselves, trying to be too many things to too many people. We feel that fallibility, that sense that we do not have it under control, that our flaws will certainly show themselves and make it difficult for us to perform. We know that we are educated or strong or have even handled similar circumstances before, but that sense of helplessness can creep in all too often, making it hard to see things clearly.

For me and for others, prayer is entirely spiritual. It is done in quiet and with the presence of mind that I am speaking to God. The need for God's help can hit us at any time. We can be challenged beyond our ability at work. A father can be overwhelmed by the actions of a wayward teen. A bad doctor's report can bring one face-to-face with mortality. The strongest man can reach the end of his strength, yet not be at the end of his responsibility. I have been there on several occasions. Reaching God through prayer has been my salvation. His guidance, protection, his care, and when necessary, his comfort have sustained me.

Many times, we understand what we need to do in life, but we need to touch base with God so that He can regulate us or allow us to take that deep breath and disclose what bothers us, what makes us happy, and what challenges us. Sometimes, there is no one else who can provide us that objective view of life. We must talk to God in prayer to understand our roles in this life and to see clearly how to handle all of them. As we have stated before, men wear many hats. We must and should perform and meet our responsibilities. A good man, father, husband, employee, employer, son, brother, and friend needs help from above from time to time, if only for assurance. There is a Gospel song written by the late Walter Hawkins that really solidifies the above point. When I was a young lad in the junior choir, it was one of the first songs for which I was selected to do the lead vocal. Ah, I long for the days when I could sing. (I digress.) The song is entitled, "Dear Jesus, I love you." Here are a few of the lyrics:

> *Dear Jesus I love you. You're a friend of mine.*
>
> *You supply my every need. My hungry soul you feed.*
>
> *I'm aware you are my source from which all blessings flow*
>
> *And with this thought in mine I know just where to go.*

That is prayer. That is power.

We must talk to God in prayer to understand our roles in this life and to see clearly how to handle all of them.

The power of prayer also allows me to be present when I am absent. I love my family. They are, however, spread out across the country. I love my friends, and when any of them are in need, I would like to be there for them. My kids live and work in another state. My daughter is a true global citizen. Earlier in the evening of this writing, I prayed for her on the telephone as she was at the airport to leave the country on vacation. Within a couple of months of this writing, she will go live abroad for a year. Although my children are young adults, I would like to protect them every second of their lives. Even though I can't be there for everybody I love all the time, I am secure in the fact that I pray for God's watchful eye over them all. I pray for my children daily and not just for their present lives. I pray for their future marriages and their spouses yet to be revealed and children yet to be born. My prayers will affect my children for years to come.

I know some of you will ask how I know that prayers for my friends and family will affect them for years to come. Obviously, my practice in prayer will affect me, but it is a harder sell to convince everyone that those you pray for are also affected. Beyond the premise that we all pray to get answers to our greater questions or to obtain peace of mind or a closer relationship with ourselves and with God, we do pray to be given strength to help friends and family and to have the presence of mind to know that they are doing well and OK. Further, we may even ask for assistance in how to help them or for God to watch over them, as He does for us. In this way, we can all feel better and, by keeping these people on your radar and in your thoughts when you pray and approach God, you keep them on your personal radar and in your often busy world.

In this and other ways, I do feel that I stay in touch with my feelings and with the feelings of others. In my own disciplined way, I stay close to God as well and tap into what I need to do to shoot for success. In this way, I am a real man—a real Christian man who prays and handles his responsibilities. I am present and aware of everywhere that I am needed or expected. As a result of how grounded prayer makes me, I relish all of my responsibilities, and I keep my friends and family covered, even if from afar. In all these ways, I am an example of a real man, and if you have not taken that step yourselves, I urge you to do so, no matter your gender, your profession, your age, your lifestyle, or your religion.

Given all that I've said about being a real man and prayer, I'd like to now touch on something else about real men in today's society that also commands my attention. This is not a phenomenon that I find on a bumper sticker, mind you, but rather in the churches, neighborhoods, schools, and playgrounds everywhere. The issue that I am faced with almost daily is that of the absentee father. Let me say emphatically, real men should be present. Much has been written on the subject. It has been studied and documented ad nauseam. Now, I would like to assume that all my engaged and interested readers are men and women who are truly active parents in general who want to be involved in the lives of their children. We just touched on parenting and how prayer can help us in that area even from far away, but I would like to spend some time encouraging brothers and sisters to show up in your kids' lives where you are needed, wherever that might be. I know most of you are saying right now that you feel you do that already. You're making the money, providing the meals, and watching every move they make to keep them on the straight and narrow and their own pathways to success. I am suggesting, however, that we do more.

If we take time out of our own lives to pray for our children, then we can certainly take time to really be there for our kids. If they need us to help them at home for homework, then we need to stop what we're doing, sit with them, and get them through whatever challenges they are encountering. We need to tap into their experience, and sitting to do homework with them can provide that perfect opportunity. At that time, you can ask about their days and find out what they truly think or feel (or even worry about and more) while they are away from you for so many hours during the day. In addition to that, the only way to get to know their friends and celebrate their accomplishments is through school functions, sporting events, youth church and civic events, and more. It is eye-opening and completely enriching to open yourself to the world of those for whom you care so much. You will never get a second chance to raise your children. There is a short window of time. It seems long, but it isn't. Trust me, I know. My children are young adults and middle school seems like only yesterday. No matter how much money you spend, presence matters. Fathers can be certain that their children need them. I wrote some lyrics years ago that express my feelings on the subject.

> *No need to try and figure what you need because what you need is me*
>
> *Never should you be left alone for it's already known*
>
> *That my presence makes a difference, a difference that can be measured*
>
> *Presence makes a difference. It's wanted and treasured*
>
> *Presence makes a difference that's why it is my pleasure to be here*
>
> *I'm here. I'm here.*

Take this with you, whether you are male or female: male presence is irreplaceable. There is no substitute for it. Whether it is the husband and father in the home, or the actively engaged father outside of the home, the coach in the athletic program, or the administrator in the school system, when a good man is present, there is tremendous value added. Every good man needs to know and remember that, to his family and community, his presence matters and his absence is a problem. Prayer and presence of mind can work wonders for making sure that we all stay in the present and be the best that we can be for ourselves, our God, and our friends and families.

Male presence is irreplaceable.
There is no substitute for it.

In prayer, ask yourselves what you can do for your spouse, your parents, and even your friends. Do you have a friend who never has anyone with whom to go to the gym? Make yourself available to that person and help yourself with a workout as well. During that workout, get to know them, spend some time talking, or try to set up a weekly night out. Maybe you've always been curious about the opera, but you have never gone. Make it a point to take someone you love, maybe a spouse, an elderly single parent, or your teenager, and take that person to the ballet or to a new restaurant. Soak in that new experience and spend time with that person with whom you should be connecting constantly and reflect on it later in prayer when you can process your good experience and apply it to other aspects of life. Learn to always be there in heart, mind, and body.

RELATIONSHIP BREAK **EIGHT**

The Power of Prayer and Truly "Being There" for People

Relationships require commitment and accountability. Your family and friends should be able to count on you for prayer and presence. Make a list of the people to which you hold yourself accountable for prayer and presence.

_____

_____

_____

_____

_____

_____

_____

How will you maintain your commitment? Make sure you are not overextending yourself.

_____

_____

_____

_____

_____

How will you demonstrate and/or communicate that commitment?

_____

_____

_____

_____

_____

_____

CHAPTER **NINE**

A Retrospective and a Work Plan

In the first few chapters of the book, we did discuss at length the idea that men have to be "on" all the time; they have to have their careers in line, their families taken care of, and their personal lives in order from fitness to financial. It is daunting, to say the least. I firmly believe, however, that we are all equipped to handle it all. We just need to get ourselves organized, and we need to prioritize and apply discipline, even in small parts, to every area of our lives. In this way, we can be universally successful.

CHAPTER ONE RETROSPECTIVE:
GETTING TOUGH WITH YOURSELF

I asked many things of my readers in Chapter One. I asked you to take stock of your lives and decide where you needed to make changes in order to reach your full potential and see your dreams and visions for yourself come to fruition. Detail below what those changes or improvements will be as you complete this book.

_____

_____

_____

_____

_____

_____

_____

I also asked all of you to evaluate your physical well-being and get yourselves on a track to physical fitness or a deepened knowledge about your own health in terms of family history, medical past, and food and fitness choices. What steps have you taken so far to improve your health and what steps will you take in the future to implement these changes? Or, what health regime do you follow now that seems to work for you? Detail it all below and at the close of your analysis, include your start date for this new plan, or provide a date on which you will re-evaluate and gauge your progress either from the past or from your new plan:

_____

_____

_____

_____

I have provided you with many sayings and philosophies. Based on what you have read and digested in this book, what is your new philosophy moving forward in life? Keep it clear and succinct:

_____

_____

_____

_____

CHAPTER TWO RETROSPECTIVE: WHO ARE YOU?

As we began to delve further into our specific areas of improvement, I did ask all of you to evaluate your finances. Below, I'd like you to talk about what you do that is good in terms of planning for retirement or trips or kids' college funds. I would like you to also talk about where you need to improve in terms of spending and saving, from credit cards to bank accounts:

_____

_____

In our lives, we need to make sure that we leave behind a legacy of sorts. Doing so requires involvement now. What are you doing to make that happen since reading about how men need to have a voice in this society? Have you taken steps to get involved in the community or with your church or even more deeply at work? If so, go ahead and talk about that here. If not, think about what you need to do or what you want to do and jot your thoughts down here—again, along with a date to start the initiative:

_____

_____

_____

As we resolve to be more financially responsible, please describe your present financial situation. Presently, what are your specific financial needs? What are your present financial goals? Write out your plan to reach those goals. If you need help, seek out a professional personal finance manager.

_____

_____

_____

Involvement is a key component of a real man's life. Presence makes a difference. What is your "commitment" plan? List the people and causes that can count on your involvement.

_____

_____

_____

_____

_____

_____

What is your understanding of being a "regular guy"? Relate your thoughts (below) to family, career, community, and church:

_____

_____

_____

_____

CHAPTER THREE RETROSPECTIVE:
THE TRUTH—AND YOUR ROLE IN IT!

Very simply, what does truth mean to you? Are you truthful? How important is it for you to be truthful and trusted as such? Detail here what you've learned as you examine all the areas in your life that need improvement or that need some TRUTH:

_____

_____

_____

_____

A good communicator must be a good listener. Listening is a skill and a discipline. The more disciplined we are in practicing active listening, the better at it we will be. List the key relationships and the important areas of your life and career in where you are a good listener:

_____

_____

_____

_____

Under what circumstances and with what people do you tend to be a poor listener? What is your improvement plan?

_____

_____

_____

_____

_____

_____

As substantive men we need to be committed or at least lend support to causes in our lives. To what cause have you lent a hand lately or volunteered time? If you haven't done that yet, detail your future plans here and provide that all important start date:

_____

_____

_____

_____

CHAPTER FOUR RETROSPECTIVE:
DO YOU HAVE A CLUE?

When was the last time you sat back and actually listened to what someone else was saying? And, further, when was the last time that you actually sought out a class, a lecture, a movie, or a book that did not fit the "norm" in terms of what you usually choose? In other words, when was the last time you stepped out of your comfort zone and tried to learn something new? Detail this experience below, including what you learned from it. If you do not have such an experience in your recent past, detail your plans to get something on your calendar below. Talk about what you hope to learn or gain from the experience:

_____

_____

_____

_____

_____

_____

_____

Also, what are your known strengths or areas of expertise? List them. Describe them and don't hold back. Now is your time to brag. You may even get additional insight on your talents, skills, and abilities.

_____

_____

_____

_____

CHAPTER FIVE RETROSPECTIVE:
DO YOU REALLY HAVE PLANS FOR THE FUTURE?

We all have plans for the future. What are your truly BIG plans? Think about vacations you want to take, jobs you want to have, and personal goals you want to reach. Now, take each of those (keep your list to two or three BIG ones) and tell us (and yourself) here HOW exactly you are planning to achieve these lofty goals and ambitions:

_____

_____

_____

What does enlightenment mean to you? Can you obtain it anywhere? A Church book? A political lecture? An exercise class? A TED talk? Think about where you find enlightenment and write about that ONE special place here. Include at the end of your analysis what type of book or other reference you might use to further your enlightenment in your chosen area:

_____

_____

_____

_____

CHAPTER SIX RETROSPECTIVE:
WHAT DO OTHERS SEE WHEN THEY LOOK AT YOU?

Were you ever on a team? In high school? At work? Think hard about when you were either a member of a team and your role on that team or when you had to collaborate with others in some way and how you contributed. Detail your specific roles and contributions here:

_____

_____

_____

_____

_____

_____

_____

_____

This might sound simplistic, but how do you feel about your wardrobe and your personal grooming? If you had to communicate to someone—maybe a younger mentee or one of your teenage children—how to present oneself in terms of style and look, what would you say? What is important to you? Talk here about how you present yourself. Are there changes you want or have to make in your grooming and style? Do you need help?

_____

_____

_____

_____

_____

CHAPTER SEVEN RETROSPECTIVE:
ARE YOU PREPARED FOR ANYTHING?

Each year, when you approach Martin Luther King Day, do you ever think about what his legacy means to you and your family? Would you be prepared, like he was, to fight for what you believe? If you had to choose something to fight for, could you compartmentalize that into one thing—one cohesive, directed cause? Try to picture that now and detail it below:

_____

_____

_____

_____

Was there ever a time in your life when you felt ill prepared for something? How did that make you feel? Detail those feelings here along with how you will keep that from ever happening again:

_____

_____

_____

_____

What do you need to do now to prepare for your future and your many roles as a man? First, decide what all those roles are and try to anticipate what may happen in the future. Next, try to come up with a plan for preparedness in all areas of your life. Choose four that are a priority to you (financial, personal, spiritual, emotional, physical, etc.) and detail them below:

_____

_____

_____

_____

CHAPTER EIGHT RETROSPECTIVE:
WHAT'S GOING ON WITH YOU PRESENT DAY?

This is a time to take a good look at your present use of time, energy, and effort. Please answer the following questions as relative to your activities, priorities, and relationships: What are you working on? (Plans, projects, self)

_____

_____

WHEN I BECAME A MAN

1. What are you working with? (What's in your toolbox?)

_____

_____

_____

2. Who are you working for? (Whom do you benefit? Whom do you answer to?)

_____

_____

_____

3. Who are you working with? (Who are your partners in your priorities?)

_____

_____

_____

4. What are you working through? (What are the lingering internal or external issues or challenges?)

_____

_____

_____

_____

Now comes the time for you to detail for yourselves and for your future plans what you've learned in this book. I don't want an overview of each chapter, and I don't want a trite one or two lines of what you plan to change in your future. I want, instead, a full three-paragraph biography of YOU. The first paragraph should be your past—where you've been, who you've been, the mistakes you've made, and the high points that stand out in your minds. The second paragraph should be your present day self—the family you have or don't have, the career you have and the subsequent issues in your life from your spiritual life, beliefs, disciplines and rituals, to your life with friends and your neighborhood, or your hobbies and traditions, and more. The third paragraph should be your future plans—specifically, your reasonable projection of what you think your life CAN be in terms of money, love, God, self, family, relationships, and more. Take your time with this. Make a list outline and make sure that you get all your thoughts down. This will be your compass for your sense of past, your sense of present-day self, and your sense of future success and happiness.

_____

_____

_____

_____

_____

_____

_____

_____

_____

_____

_____

_____

CHAPTER NINE

WHEN I BECAME A MAN

ABOUT THE **AUTHOR**

Derek T. Triplett is an esteemed pastor, author, urban youth mentor, radio personality, and, above all, a change agent.

He is a consecrated Bishop in the Lord's Church and Founding Pastor of Hope Fellowship Church in Daytona Beach, Florida. In his capacity as a sought-after guest speaker and community mentor, he serves as the ecclesiastical and spiritual covering for several well-known churches, ministries, and pastors throughout the United States.

With his passion for community transformation and empowerment, Triplett serves the community in numerous civic capacities and has received several awards. A strong advocate for urban youth, Bishop Triplett is the founder of Getting All Males Equipped (G.A.M.E.), a male mentoring and development initiative. G.A.M.E. presents forums to help shape the minds of urban males so they may learn to make good decisions, change negative behavior patterns, and build proper standards for effective living.

He is a longtime media personality, and is currently the host of Making Changes with Derek Triplett, a radio broadcast which airs weekly on several stations. He also hosts a relationship segment on Fox 35 Orlando. An experienced composer, Triplett has released two albums to date and has several other recording credits.

ABOUT THE AUTHOR

Triplett is a graduate of Bradley University in Peoria, Illinois. He has studied at Reformed Theological Seminary in Orlando, Florida and is also a graduate of Leadership Daytona, a program designed for active community leaders.

He is the proud father of two phenomenal children, Destanni and Donovan.

For more information on Derek Triplett, please visit his website at www.derektriplett.com.